The Flavours and Scents of Rome

TRADITIONAL ROMAN CUISINE: RECIPES AND RESTAURANTS

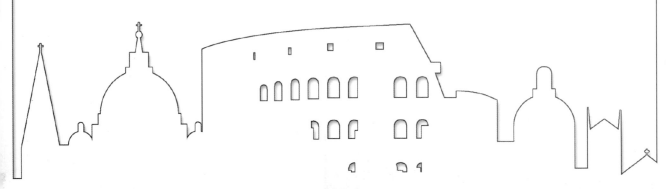

L'ORTENSIA ROSSA

As you flip through these pages you will find pictures and recipes that will tempt you to try a variety of Roman dishes. If you like cooking, you will thoroughly enjoy discovering this style of Italian cuisine and its own special nuances.

Over and above the recipes, you will truly "taste" the feeling of Rome: the book is enriched with photos of some of the most beautiful sites in the city and presentations of "trattorias" and traditional Roman restaurants that prepare the recipes presented here.

THE RECIPES
- The recipes include APPETIZERS, FIRST COURSES, SECOND COURSES, SIDE DISHES AND DESSERTS
- The recipes make 4 servings
- The ingredients are generally easy to find and we have suggested possible substitutions when necessary.

THE WINES
The recipes have been paired with 27 DOC (Controlled Designation of Origin) wines produced around Rome and Lazio.

TRADITIONAL RESTAURANTS
The 35 establishments listed include restaurants and trattorias which were chosen according to
- quality
- location
- traditional Roman style
- average price (around 30 Euros per person, excluding drinks).

L'ORTENSIA ROSSA SRL (LOZZI GROUP)
Circ. Gianicolense 210 - 00152 Rome • Tel.: +39 0698387080-1-2-3 • Fax: +39 065349779 • E-mail: info@ortensiarossa.it

GRAPHIC DESIGN AND LAYOUT: Line Art Studio (Roma) • AUTHOR: Silvia Guglielmi • EDITORIAL STAFF: Francesca Faramondi, Laura Cavallo
Translation: Bonnie Jeanne Nielsen • © Subject to copyright L'Ortensia Rossa srl - Full or partial copying is prohibited

QUADERNI DELL'ORTENSIA ROSSA (I) - ISSN 2035-9578 - Monthly periodical - Court of Rome registration no. 18/2009 dated 16/01/2009
Managing director: Silvia Guglielmi - Printed by ARTI GRAFICHE AGOSTINI (Anagni)
1st edition June 2010 - 2nd edition March 2011 - 3rd edition November 2011 - 4rd edition April 2012 - 5rd edition May 2013

APPETIZERS

Roman cuisine is authentic and traditional from the appetizers to the desserts. The primary aim of the recipes was to provide tasty and hearty dishes from less expensive ingredients, which were filling after a hard day of labour. In fact some classic traditional appetizers can serve as a quick and complete meal for those of us who lead more sedentary lives.

Fried foods triumph. This simple cooking method, which requires some attention, gives rise to some of Roman cuisine's best recipes. Stringy mozzarella is another characteristic ingredient that makes these simple dishes even better.

The irresistible bruschetta is a truly frugal dish. In olden days it was only considered as a "snack" for those who worked outside: farmers, shepherds, woodsmen... It remains a perfect choice for beginning a meal, and it is great accompanied by a glass of wine from the nearby Castelli Romani hills: there could be no better way to prepare your palate for the flavourful dishes that follow.

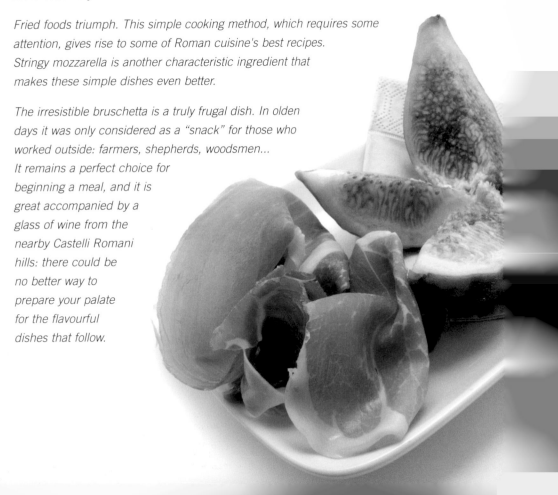

› SANTA MARIA IN TRASTEVERE

TRADITIONAL RESTAURANTS

AI SPAGHETTARI

› Piazza S. Cosimato, 57-60
  (S. Maria in Trastevere)
› Tel.: 06 5800450 - www.aispaghettari.it
› Closed: Mondays and Tuesdays at lunch
› Average price (excluding drinks): Euro 30,00

In the heart of Rome's Trastevere district near the church of Santa Maria in Trastevere, there is a very old establishment that has been under the same management since 1896: "Ai Spaghettari". The restaurant's cuisine is rooted in classic Roman culinary traditions and in the evenings they also serve classic Roman thin crust pizza. The restaurant is open until late and during the milder seasons there is an open-air garden available as well.
Specialties: lamb, amatriciana-style pasta, bruschetta, carbonara-style pasta, oxtail stew, crostini, "supplì" rice croquettes

Bruschetta
Bruschetta

› 8 slices of day-old crusty bread;
› 2-3 garlic cloves;
› extra virgin olive oil and salt to taste.

 QUICK   EASY

THE HISTORY OF THE DISH

This very simple appetizer is a favourite that never grows old. A humble and traditional dish that has many regional variations, it can be topped in lots of creative ways. It is however of utmost importance that you use high quality olive oil.

DIRECTIONS

Toast the bread (over a wood fire if possible). Rub garlic on each slice of bread and then place it on a warm plate and top with salt and a generous serving of oil. The tomato bruschetta is a much loved variation: after adding the garlic and oil simply top each slice with tomatoes (not too ripe) cut into chunks and add a little salt and chopped basil.

RECOMMENDED WINE

TERRACINA (DOC)
A recently appointed DOC wine, Moscato di Terracina (or simply Terracina) has ancient and noble origins.
In fact, the vine was brought into the land of Magna Grecia by settlers from Ionia and Samos.
Its magnificent reputation along the coast of Lazio Pontine is celebrated by Homer, who mentions the heady wine which the sorceress Circe enchants visitors with. This wine is offered, fragrant and fresh as the perfect combination for sweet and sour dishes, in sparkling, dry, sweet and passito versions, it is a perfect companion from starter to dessert.

Crostini con mozzarella e alici

Crostini with mozzarella and anchovies

› 250 g of fresh mozzarella;
› 100 g of butter;
› 12 slices of Italian bread or a baguette cut into squares measuring around 5 cm per side;
› 8 anchovies (rinsed of salt);
› milk, salt and pepper to taste.

 MEDIUM   EASY

THE CUISINE OF ANCIENT ROME

The ancient Romans ate three meals per day.
In the morning they started with a light breakfast (jentaculum) made up of bread and cheese.
At noon they ate a light lunch (prandium) including bread, cold meat, fruit and wine, which they frequently ate while standing.
The main meal of the day was dinner (coena), which began between 3 and 4 pm and sometimes lasted until dawn the next day.
The dinner was divided into three major courses: appetizers and snacks (gustatio); the actual meal (primae mensae) which generally included seven dishes; and the desserts (secundae mensae). The evening would continue with a symposium where watered wine was accompanied by savoury dishes that encouraged thirst.
These "savoury dishes" were meats (generally pork, but fowl and larger game such as wild boar and venison were also enjoyed). One of the main characteristics of Roman cuisine was the pairing of contrasting flavours (such as hot-spicy and sweet). Today we would turn up our noses at many of those recipes such as boiled pears with honey, raisins, fish sauce, oil and egg which was a delicacy at the most refined tables.

THE HISTORY OF THE DISH

The original recipe for these delicious appetizers called for "provatura" instead of mozzarella. "Provatura", which is the delicious cheese created before making mozzarella, used to be available in the Lazio and Campania regions. In Italian "prova" means to try or test, and 'provatura' was the portion of the cheese they extracted to test whether the consistency and grain of the curd was ready to form the mozzarella. It is not easy to find unless you know an artisan cheese maker.

DIRECTIONS

Cut the mozzarella into 12 thick slices and dress them with salt and pepper. Alternate slices of bread and mozzarella on skewers and then bake at 200°. In the meantime melt the butter in a pan on a low heat and sauté the anchovies (mixing well) until they fall apart. If necessary add a little milk in order to form a cream.
When the bread is crunchy and the mozzarella has melted, remove the skewers from the oven and cover them with the anchovy cream. Serve hot.

› RIPA GRANDE FOUNTAIN

TRADITIONAL RESTAURANTS

SAN MICHELE

› Time consumingtevere Ripa, 7 (Ripa Grande)
› Tel.: 06 5844826
  www.ristorantesanmichele.com
  info@ristorantesanmichele.com
› Closed: Sundays
› Average price (excluding drinks): Euro 30,00

Enchanted with Rome, America's first lady Michelle Obama dined at San Michele, a traditional Roman trattoria located on Time consumingtevere Ripa along the Tiber River. This restaurant-pizzeria has an ample terrace and garden, San Michele seems like a splendid sun room for tasting traditional dishes in the open air without having to breathe the smog from the city traffic. Specialties: zucchini flowers

 MEDIUM   AVERAGE

Fiori di zucca fritti
Fried zucchini flowers

› 600 g of fresh zucchini blossoms;
› 6 anchovies (rinse to remove salt);
› 150 g of mozzarella;
› 100 g of flour;
› 2 egg whites;
› parsley, extra-virgin olive oil and salt to taste.

THE HISTORY OF THE DISH

In the rich tradition of regional fried foods, this tasty delight sets itself apart for its correlation with springtime and its tasty filling.

DIRECTIONS

Prepare the batter by mixing 1 cup of water, the flour, a little salt and 2 tablespoons of olive oil: the batter should be quite dense. Let the batter rest for one hour. In the meantime prepare the filling by mixing the mozzarella (cut into chunks), the sliced anchovies and diced parsley. Carefully open each blossom and fill it with some of the filling and then pinch it closed. Whip the egg whites into a meringue and add it to the batter. Then dip the filled blossoms into the batter and carefully remove them before deep frying until they turn golden brown on both sides. Use a slotted spoon to remove the blossoms from the oil and then lay them on paper towels to absorb any excess oil before serving.

RECOMMENDED WINE

CERVETERI (DOC)

The production area is located along a hilly coastal strip of the Tuscia area north of Rome in the ancient lands of the Etruscans. There are many archaeological testimonies which demonstrate that vineyards were very important to the Etruscan economy in this territory. The white pairs well with seafood, fava beans and artichokes, and fresh cheeses. The red goes well with cold cuts, first courses with flavourful sauces, roasted chicken, goat and grilled or roasted wether, roasts and lamb cacciatore. The rosé is a good dinner wine and it pairs best with cold cuts, soups, mild cheeses, fried zucchini flowers and egg dishes.

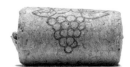

Panzerotti alla Romana

Savoury Roman pastries

- › 300 g of flour;
- › 120 g of Scamorza (or Gruyere) cheese;
- › 70 g of sugar-cured ham (*prosciutto cotto*) cut into chunks (optional);
- › 3 eggs;
- › 50 g of butter;
- › extra virgin olive oil and salt to taste.

 MEDIUM   EASY

THE HISTORY OF THE DISH

Great as appetizers or snacks, they can be enriched as you like depending on your preferences or inspiration.

DIRECTIONS

Pour the flour into a fountain shape and form a well at the centre. Place the egg yolks into the indention and set the egg whites aside. Then add the butter (in pieces), some salt, and water and knead the mixture until it is solid and the texture is consistent. Form a dough ball, cover it with a towel and let it rise for half an hour. Then roll out the dough to form a thin to medium width sheet. Cut round dough circles (from 8 to 12 cm in diameter). Place the cheese cut into chunks at the centre, then add the ham and a little salt. Brush the edges of the dough circles with beaten egg white and fold the circles in half taking care to close the ends well. Deep fry the pastries in hot oil until the dough has turned golden brown on both sides.

TRADITIONAL RESTAURANTS

IL FALCHETTO

› Via dei Montecatini, 12/14
  (Trevi Fountain)
› Tel.: 06 5844826
  www.ristoranteilfalchetto.it
  info@ristoranteilfalchetto.it
› Closed: Fridays
› Average price (excluding
  drinks): Euro 30,00

After having thrown a coin into the Trevi Fountain to secure your return to Rome, stop in and have a bite at Falchetto.

The establishment is made up of a large hall and two small adjacent rooms. When the weather is nice there are also tables for outdoor dining.

Here you can try all of the classic dishes of Roman tradition, accompanied by local wines.

Specialties: tripe

Supplì di riso

Rice croquettes

› 300-400 g of rice;
› 500 ml of tomato sauce with meat;
› 1-3 eggs;
› 40 g of grated parmesan;
› 1 small fresh mozzarella;
› flour (optional), bread crumbs, extra virgin olive oil to taste.

MEDIUM	AVERAGE

THE HISTORY OF THE DISH

In Sicily they prepare a very similar specialty called an "arancino". Everybody loves these croquettes which are affectionately referred to in Italy as "telephone cord croquettes" because when they are broken in half the mozzarella forms a long string that runs from one end to the other. The original recipe can be varied by adding peas or pieces of salt-cured ham to the filling.

DIRECTIONS

Prepare a risotto with a tomato and meat sauce using crushed herbs and ground beef (you can also use chopped chicken livers). If you prefer you can boil the rice and top it with the sauce: the important thing is that in either case, the rice needs to be cooked "al dente". Top the rice with parmesan and when it has cooled, add 1 beaten egg. Form oval croquettes and place a piece of mozzarella at the centre of each of them. There are two methods for breading the croquettes. You can either roll each croquette delicately in bread crumbs, or roll them in flour, then beaten egg and then bread crumbs. Fry a few at a time in a tall pan with lots of oil, carefully stirring only once. They should be served piping hot while the mozzarella is still stringy.

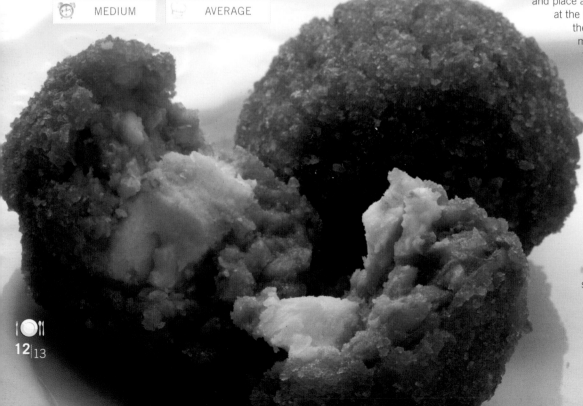

FIRST COURSES

Traditional Roman first courses absolutely mirror the people of Lazio's passion for traditional and intense flavours.

They include hearty soups and stews - classics based on legumes or highly original dishes such as the unusual but absolutely tasty combination of pasta and broccoli with rayfish - as well as appetizing quick pasta dishes or pasta topped with amazing meat sauces.

There is also an abundance of delicate flavours, such as "fettucine alla papalina" or "gnocchi di semolina" but hearty ingredients are definitely more common, such as: cured pork (lard, bacon, pork jowl), the intense flavours of garlic and hot pepper, and above all the final touch is provided by sharp pecorino romano cheese - currently protected by a DOP label - which has been produced in the Agro Romano area since the days of the Roman Empire.

Bucatini all'Amatriciana

Amatrice-style bucatini

› 500 g of bucatini pasta (type of thick spaghetti);
› 125 g of pork jowl;
› 1 tablespoon of extra-virgin olive oil;
› dry white wine for flavour;
› 6 or 7 San Marzano tomatoes or 400 g of canned tomatoes;
› one hot pepper;
› 100 g of grated pecorino cheese;
› salt to taste.

THE HISTORY OF THE DISH

The meek lamb and the good pig together gave cheese and pork jowl... (C. Baccarà).

These are the two simple ingredients that shepherds in Abruzzo would use to top their frugal yet substantial single course pasta meals. Amatrice is a smiling city in the Upper Sabina area, which is currently part of the province of Rieti. However in the past, it was part of Aquila, and therefore part of Abruzzo. This simple pastoral recipe developed into one of the most famous Italian specialties thanks to the fact that this ancient recipe met with tomatoes in Amatrice. It was no accident, on 28 February 1529, the Spaniards razed the city to the ground and Amatrice became part of the Kingdom of Naples. The Neapolitans were among the first to recognise the qualities of the tomato at the end of the 1700s, which gave the people of Amatrice a chance to try them - and they had the excellent idea of adding tomato to pecorino cheese and pork jowl to make a succulent and brilliant pasta sauce, which has crossed Italian borders to be affirmed internationally.

DIRECTIONS

Put the oil, hot pepper and diced pork jowl in a skillet (preferably iron). Tradition dictates and experts say that the golden proportion of pasta to pork jowl is four to one. Only by using "guanciale" or un-smoked pork jowl bacon can you make truly delicate, tantalising Bucatini all'Amatriciana. Lightly brown the pork over a high flame and then add a little dry white wine. Remove the pork pieces from the skillet allowing them to drain well and set them aside (if possible put them in a warm place so that the pork remains soft and flavourful without becoming dry and salty). Remove the skin and seeds of the tomato (or drop them in boiling water for a moment to remove the skin more easily, and then cut them) and add to the pan. Add salt for flavour, mix and cook for a few minutes. Remove the hot pepper and return the pork to the pan and stir. In the meantime boil the pasta al dente in lots of salted water. Drain the pasta and put it in a bowl and add the grated pecorino cheese. Wait a few seconds and then pour in the sauce. Mix it all, and if you like, add more pecorino.

› S. ANDREA DELLA VALLE - DOME

TRADITIONAL RESTAURANTS

DER PALLARO

› Largo del Pallaro, 15 (Corso Vittorio)
› Tel.: 06 68801488 - www.trattoriaderpallaro.com
› Closed: Mondays
› Average price (excluding drinks): Euro 25,00

After having visited the lovely Sant'Andrea della Valle Church, a stop at "Der Pallaro" is a must. This classic Roman establishment is all about 'the more the better'. There is a fixed price set menu and there is no ordering; you get the specialty of the day. The environment is simple and uncomplicated with informal and courteous service. The simple traditional dishes are all made by hand and accompanied with house wine.
Specialties: amatriciana-style pasta, carbonara-style pasta, gricia-style pasta, "puntarelle" chicory salad

Fettuccine alla Papalina

"Papal" fettuccine

› 400-500 g of fresh egg fettuccine;
› 1/2 an onion (chopped finely);
› 200 ml of cream;
› 100 g of salt-cured ham cut into chunks;
› 3 eggs;
› 200 g of fresh or frozen peas;
› 100 g of grated parmesan cheese;
› butter, salt and pepper to taste.

 MEDIUM   EASY

VIP PASTA

220 years have passed since Thomas Jefferson introduced pasta to the United States after having a macaroni press sent from Naples. 161 years have passed since an Italian immigrant opened the first pasta factory in Brooklyn. Today pasta brings Italy to mind all over the world, but it is a dish that is famous and celebrated everywhere. World Pasta Day is an event dedicated to this food that symbolizes the Mediterranean diet, but which has become a basic element in kitchens in all five continents.

Pasta is a typical part of tasty Roman dishes that are deliciously irresistible and sometimes a little unique. Hollywood stars and the restaurants they visit when they come to Italy can serve as testimony.

Tom Hanks and De Niro love pasta "alla carbonara". Former first lady Laura Bush, Hugh Grant and Penelope Cruz find "cacio e pepe" irresistible, while Leonardo Di Caprio cannot resist pasta "all'Amatriciana".

THE HISTORY OF THE DISH

This dish has historic origins: it was perfected in the 30s by a cook from the working class Borgo neighbourhood of Rome to satisfy the palates of Cardinal Pacelli and then Pope Pius XII. That is how this "aristocratic" version of the more typical pasta carbonara was born. The ingredients are richer and more refined, and the flavour is more delicate. Purists say that the original recipe did not contain peas, but they are a nice colourful addition and they have been a common ingredient for some time.

DIRECTIONS

Melt the butter in a pan over a medium flame. Add the onion and ham, and after a few minutes add the peas, salt and cook for 10 minutes. Turn the stove off; add the beaten eggs, the parmesan cheese and delicately mix it all together. In the meantime boil the fettuccine, drain and pour it into the pan together with the topping. Stir and top with fresh grated pepper before serving.

Gnocchi di patate

Potato gnocchi (dumplings)

› 2 kg of floury potatoes;
› 400 g of sifted flour;
› 1/2 litre of tomato meat sauce (or simple tomato sauce with onion and tomatoes);
› 120 g of grated parmesan cheese, salt to taste.

DIRECTIONS

Boil the potatoes whole. Peel and mash them as soon as they are cool. Add the flour to the mashed potatoes while they are still warm. The dough will be thick, but delicate and soft.

Divide the dough into pieces and flour your hands before rolling out 2.5 cm diameter dough logs. Cut the logs into pieces around 3 cm long and gently press them in the centre with your index and middle finger. Lay the gnocchi individually on a flour covered surface avoiding that they touch. It is best to prepare the dough at the last minute as it is quite susceptible to humidity.

Pour the gnocchi into a large pan of boiling salted water and when they rise to the surface, remove them with a slotted spoon and set

them on a serving plate. Wait a few seconds then add a few spoonfuls of parmesan cheese and half of the sauce. Serve hot topped with the rest of the sauce and parmesan.

RECOMMENDED WINE

APRILIA (DOC)
This young DOC wine is produced in Aprilia and surrounding areas in the province of Latina. The land where the grapes are grown is primarily of volcanic or alluvial origin.
The Merlot is perfect for pairing with strong flavoured first courses (gnocchi alla romana, bucatini alla carbonara and meat sauces), white or red meats and aged cheeses; the Sangiovese is great with full bodied spicy flavours, and with mushrooms.
The Trebbiano is ideal with fish, seafood or crustaceans, and vegetable dishes.

TRADITIONAL RESTAURANTS

TRATTORIA ZAMPAGNA
› Via Ostiense, 179 (Saint Paul Outside the Walls)
› Tel.: 06 5742306
› Closed: Sundays. Not open for lunch.
› Average price (excluding drinks): Euro 25,00

Trattoria Zampagna is located behind the Basilica of Saint Paul Outside the Walls and it is a classic trattoria of days gone by: furnished with a few tables and paper tablecloths, the environment is polite and informal. The menu is recited by the waiter and it follows the typical Roman schedule with gnocchi on Thursdays, codfish on Fridays and tripe on Saturdays.
Specialties: codfish, cacio e pepe-style pasta, carbonara-style pasta, oxtail stew, gnocchi, gricia-style pasta, roulade, tripe

> SYNAGOGUE

TRADITIONAL RESTAURANTS

SORA MARGHERITA

› Piazza delle Cinque Scole, 30 (Portico d'Ottavia)
› Tel.: 06 6874216
› Closed: Sundays; during the summers closed at dinner Monday through Friday; during winter months closed at lunch from Monday to Thursday
› Average price (excluding drinks): Euro 30,00

"Sora Margherita" is a simple trattoria where time seems to have stopped; the atmosphere of this restaurant located in the historic Jewish quarter, near the Synagogue, is just like the olden days as is the menu which respects all the traditions of Roman and Jewish cuisine.
Specialties: lamb, anchovies with endive, cacio e pepe-style pasta, artichokes, "coratella", ricotta pie, zucchini flowers, semolina gnocchi, pasta and broccoli with rayfish, tripe

Gnocchi di semolino alla Romana

Roman-style semolina gnocchi

› 200 g of durum semolina;
› 1 litre of milk (a little less);
› 2 eggs;
› 120 g of grated parmesan;
› butter and salt to taste.

 MEDIUM   EASY

THE HISTORY OF THE DISH

This very simple dish earns its merits from the fragrant crust of butter and cheese.

DIRECTIONS

Place the salt and milk in a pan to boil and slowly pour in the semolina and mix without interruption for around ten minutes. Remove from the flame; add 30 g of butter, 1 tablespoon of parmesan and two eggs; then mix. Pour the semolina onto a smooth cool surface and let it cool. Form diamonds with sides of around 4 centimetres. Butter a baking pan and place the semolina shapes onto it and cover them with cheese. Melt 60 g of butter and pour it over the semolina diamonds and top them once again with cheese and bake in a hot oven (200°) until they turn golden brown.

RECOMMENDED WINE

VELLETRI (DOC)
This wine is produced in the area surrounding the town of Velletri, in the zone south of the Castelli Romani up to the countryside of Cisterna di Latina. It has always been a zone of high quality wine since the days of the ancient Romans. Pliny the Elder described the local production methods in detail. In '500s it was the most popular wine in Rome. The white is ideal for appetizers, gnocchi alla romana, first courses with seafood, artichokes, roasted pork, omelettes and fresh cheeses. The red is a flexible wine that is suitable for the entire meal. The spumante versions are great for aperitifs or for accompanying delicate appetizers or the end of the meal.

Pasta e broccoli con l'arzilla (razza)

Pasta and broccoli with rayfish

  MEDIUM

AVERAGE

› 1 fresh rayfish (around 1 kg);
› 300 g of green cauliflower;
› 200 g of tomato chunks;
› 1 onion;
› 2 garlic cloves;
› 4 anchovies (rinse to remove salt);
› 1/2 glass of dry white wine;
› 200 g of broken spaghetti;
› extra virgin olive oil, hot pepper, diced parsley and salt to taste.

RECOMMENDED WINE

MONTECOMPATRI COLONNA (DOC)
This wine is produced in an area that is located inside the perimeter of the ancient Latium volcano where the city of Labicum was once located. The vineyards are located in the municipality of Colonna and the nearby towns in the province of Rome. The vineyards are located on hilly lands that are not over 480 meters in altitude. It is a dry wine that is perfect for dining. It is pleasing with egg-based appetizers, pasta with marinara sauce, seafood or vegetables, and above all with Roman or Jewish style artichokes, omelettes or seafood soups. The amabile and dolce versions are perfect dessert wines.

THE HISTORY OF THE DISH

This intensely flavoured soup has original ingredients and it is very nutritious.

DIRECTIONS

Place the cleaned rayfish on the bottom of a frying pan and fill the pan with salted water. Add garlic, onion and diced parsley. Bring to a boil and let it cook for 10 minutes. Remove the rayfish and cut it into fillets. Set the fillets apart and place the remaining pieces back into the broth to cook for another fifteen minutes; then filter the broth. Sauté the anchovies, 1 clove of garlic and the parsley in another pan. After a few minutes add the wine and let it cook until the wine evaporates. Add the mixture to the broth together with the cauliflower tips. Cook for 6-7 minutes and then add the pasta and continue cooking until the pasta is al dente.

› VATICAN MUSEUM STAIRS

TRADITIONAL RESTAURANTS

BIBI E ROMEO

› Via della Giuliana, 87-89 (Prati)
› Tel.: 06 39735650
  info@bibieromeo.it
  www.bibieromeo.it
› Closed: Saturdays and Sundays at lunch
› Average price (excluding drinks):
  Euro 30,00

After having toured the Vatican Museums, remain in the Prati district to dine simply and flavourfully at Bibi & Romeo restaurant.
The restaurant serves traditional Roman cuisine as well as many seafood specialties.
There is an ample wine list offering 100 different labels from all over Italy.
Specialities: lamb, amatriciana-style pasta, cacio e pepe-style pasta, oxtail stew, ricotta pie, gricia-style pasta, pasta and broccoli with rayfish, chicken and bell peppers, rigatoni with "pajata", tripe

› PIAZZA FARNESE FOUNTAIN

TRADITIONAL RESTAURANTS

SETTIMIO AL PELLEGRINO

› Via del Pellegrino, 117 (Piazza Farnese)
› Tel.: 06 68801978
› Closed: Wednesdays
› Average price (excluding drinks): Euro 30,00

Da Settimio serves very home style cuisine. The owner accompanies diners to their tables and then tells them the menu which varies from day to day. The atmosphere is homey and the cuisine is simple, but the dishes are prepared with care and high quality ingredients. It is located very near Palazzo Farnese.
Specialties: gnocchi, roulade, pasta and chickpeas, tripe

Pasta e ceci

Pasta and chickpeas

› 500 g of dry chickpeas (soaked overnight);
› 4 anchovies packed in oil;
› 2 garlic cloves;
› 200 g of cannolicchi or ditalini (if you cannot find these types of pasta locally, other types of short pasta are also good);
› rosemary, extra virgin olive oil, salt and pepper to taste.

 TIME CONSUMING   EASY

THE HISTORY OF THE DISH

This dish is traditionally served on days when the Catholic Church required abstinence from meat, and it is still a common Friday specialty. You can find chickpeas that have already been soaked overnight in many traditional Italian delis, known as "pizzicherie". This makes an excellent and hearty dish.

DIRECTIONS

Boil the chickpeas in a large pot of salted water with a twig of rosemary and 1 garlic clove. Allow it to cook for a couple of hours and in the meantime sauté the diced anchovies, one crushed garlic clove and another small twig of rosemary in a little olive oil. Remove the rosemary branch after cooking and add the mixture to the chickpeas when they have finished cooking. If you can, remove the rosemary from the broth as well, then add the pasta and cook until the pasta is al dente.

RECOMMENDED WINE

CESANESE
DI OLEVANO ROMANO (DOC)
This wine is produced in the Ciociaria area, which is a pre-Apennine zone between Rome and Frosinone in the municipality of Olevano and it is also produced in Genazzano. The vineyards are planted on highlands made up of limey clay and rocky soil. It pairs well with cold cuts, fettuccine, first courses with meat sauces, risotto or bean soups, grilled pork livers and other pork dishes, tripe stew, roasted chicken and rabbit, pecorino romano and other aged cheeses. The dolce and spumante versions are great with cookies, cakes, pies and traditional shortbread cookies.

RENATO E LUISA

› Via dei Barbieri, 25 (Largo Argentina)
› Tel.: 06 6869660
  info@renatoeluisa.it - www.renatoeluisa.it
› Closed: Mondays. Not open for lunch.
› Average price (excluding drinks): Euro 40,00

Very close to Largo Argentina and to the characteristic Fountain of the Turtles, "Renato e Luisa" is located on a quiet lane.
The restaurant is friendly and welcoming. The pasta, the bread and the desserts are all strictly homemade. The menu includes both Roman traditional dishes and tasty seafood specialties.
Specialties: amatriciana-style pasta, artichokes, "saltimbocca" veal slices

Penne alla Puttanesca

MEDIUM

EASY

"Puttanesca" pasta

› 400 g of penne pasta;
› 400 g of tomato chunks or fresh juicy sauce tomatoes;
› 150 g of pitted black olives;
› 2 garlic cloves;
› 6 anchovies (rinsed of salt);
› 1 spoonful of capers (rinsed);
› grated parsley, oregano, hot pepper, extra virgin olive oil and salt to taste.

› THE FOUNTAIN
  OF THE TURTLES
  PIAZZA MATTEI

THE HISTORY OF THE DISH

This delicious pasta dish belongs to both Roman and Napolitan tradition, but according to some people only the Roman recipe includes the use of anchovies. The dish has a very unusual name that translates loosely as "brothel-style pasta". Though there are many legends as to how it got this name, one of the most popular is that in the days of brothels, the "ladies of the night" were only allowed to shop at the market one day a week (so as not to offend the decency of the other shoppers). Back in the days before refrigerators, the ladies' larders were bare by the end of the week, but these ingredients were almost always on hand to feed a hungry customer. Still today, this is a dish that you can usually make without having to run to the grocery store for ingredients.

DIRECTIONS

Finely dice the anchovies, the hot pepper, the capers and the olives. Sauté the garlic with a little oil and remove the garlic pieces as soon as they become golden brown. Add the diced mixture to the oil and after a moment add the tomato (if you use fresh tomatoes: skin, deseed and cut them into pieces). Add salt and allow the mixture to cook over a high flame. Continue mixing until it has thickened a great deal. Boil the penne al dente, drain and cover it with the sauce. Add the parsley and oregano (optional) right before serving. Some people prefer to sauté the pasta for a minute in the pan together with the sauce and a ladleful of the water used to cook the pasta.

RECOMMENDED WINE

GENAZZANO (DOC)
This production area is located in the high Sacco valley in the eastern part of the Prenestini Hills. This area north of the Ciociaria zone is particularly suited to wine production thanks to its climate, its hilliness and its volcanic origin which have given rise to a high production level and high quality. The white pairs well with seafood dishes and light appetizers; the frizzante version is a great aperitif and it pairs well with delicate flavours. The red is good throughout the meal and it is great for accompanying soups, roasted meats, wild game and aged cheeses.

Rigatoni con la pajata

Rigatoni with "pajata"

› 400 g of rigatoni pasta;
› 800 g of "pajata" (suckling veal intestine or suckling lamb intestine);
› 50 g of bacon cut into pieces;
› 1 glass of dry white wine;
› 1/2 an onion, 1 carrot and 1 stalk of celery diced finely;
› 1 garlic clove;
› 1 clove;
› 500 g of tomato chunks or chopped boiled tomatoes;
› 80 g of grated pecorino romano cheese;
› 1 hot pepper;
› parsley (if desired);
› extra virgin olive oil, vinegar and salt to taste.

THE FIFTH QUARTER

The traditional foods of the Roman people were specialties created from less expensive ingredients; the portions were large if possible and very flavourful. The highpoints of this cuisine were the first courses, including pasta and soups, and the so-called "fifth quarter". The fifth quarter was the part of the animal (beef or lamb) that remained after the more valuable cuts (the two front quarters and the two hind quarters) were sold to wealthier clients. Therefore the fifth quarter included all of the edible interior and the scraps, including: tripe (the most valued part is the "omasum", which is also called the "cuffia" in Roman), the kidneys (called "rognoni" in Italian), heart, liver, spleen and sweetbreads (pancreas, thymus and salivary glands), brains, tongue and the tail. From mutton, they also use the "coratella" which includes the liver, lungs and heart. For pork and veal, this list also includes the hooves. Roman cooks and homemakers created a true universe of food from the fifth quarter. Some of the most famous Roman recipes are prepared with that which was once considered the meat of the poor: oxtail stew, rigatoni with "pajata", fried sweetbreads, roasted head, and the famous Roman-style tripe.

THE HISTORY OF THE DISH

This is probably the most unique of all Roman specialties. It was born in Testaccio where it was prepared together with other scrap cuts for the employees of the slaughterhouse who were paid in part with these lesser cuts of meat.
Due to the dangers connected with "mad cow" disease, veal intestine is no longer sold and it has been substituted with lamb intestine.

DIRECTIONS

Skin the intestine (if you are able to find lamb intestine locally, the butcher may be able to do this for you) then rinse and place in a bowl and spray it with vinegar. After half an hour cut the intestine into 15-20 cm pieces. Some people prefer to tie the ends together with kitchen string to form a doughnut shape and others prefer to leave the pieces as they are.

If you choose to tie the ends, the milk curd stays inside making the meat more tasty while if you choose the second method, the contents mix with the sauce to make it more flavourful and creamier.

Choose the method you prefer. In the meantime prepare crushed garlic, onion, celery, carrot and unsmoked bacon and allow it to sauté in a large pan. After a few minutes add the intestine and let it cook until it has browned.

Add the wine and cook until it has evaporated; then add the tomato, the clove, the hot pepper and the salt. Cook at low heat for around 3 hours (stir and add hot water if it becomes too dry). Cook the rigatoni al dente, drain and mix the pasta together quickly with the sauce. Then add pecorino romano cheese and, if you prefer, top it with parsley before serving.

RECOMMENDED WINE

CORI (DOC)
The production area of this wine is located on the Monti Lepini hills in the province of Latina covering an area of 550 hectares. The hilly area is closed by the mountains behind it and opens onto the vast Pontina plains directly in front of the sea which makes the climate milder. The vineyards are small for the most part and cultivated with traditional techniques. The grape blend is based on local vines that are wisely mixed with others of national importance. The white pairs well with fava beans, peas and artichokes soup, vegetable soups, asparagus and seafood dishes. The red is ideal for accompanying flavourful meats such as roasted and grilled goat or roasted chicken. The amabile and dolce versions are perfect with cookies, shortbreads and traditional desserts.

Riso e cicoria

Rice and chicory

› 500 g of wild chicory (well-cleaned);
› 200 g of tomato chunks;
› 80 g of grated pecorino cheese;
› 2 tablespoons of crushed celery, onion and carrot;
› 200 g of rice;
› extra virgin olive oil, salt and pepper to taste.

THE HISTORY OF THE DISH

Until recently it was common to see the "cicoriare" walking along quiet country roads. They were for the most part older women with their heads to the ground looking to harvest wild chicory plants. This gave rise to a variety of tasty vegetarian recipes made from this 'poor food' par excellence.

DIRECTIONS

Boil the wild chicory greens in salted water, drain, and then squeeze the water from them before cutting the greens into small pieces. Sauté the crushed celery, onion and carrot in a large skillet. Add the tomato sauce, salt and pepper and cook for 5 minutes stirring continuously. Add the chicory, the rice and after having sautéed the mixture, add 1/2 litre of hot water (or broth) and continue cooking until the rice is done. Top with grated pecorino cheese and serve.

RECOMMENDED WINE

CASTELLI ROMANI (DOC)

The Castelli Romani area has been the most important wine producing zone in Lazio since ancient times. The volcanic origin of the land makes it perfect thanks to the composition of the soil, which is rich in potassium and phosphorus, and also thanks to the climate which is eased by the nearby lakes and the nearness to the sea. Castelli Romani DOC is produced in twenty municipalities in the province of Rome and in a few surrounding communities in the province of Latina. The white wine pairs well with most first courses, including seafood rice or pasta and risotto with vegetables. The red is great with roasts or grilled beef, chicken or even rabbit cacciatore. The rosé variety pairs well with any meal.

› PORTA PORTESE MARKET

TRADITIONAL RESTAURANTS

OSTERIA FERNANDA

› Via Ettore Rolli, 1 (Porta Portese)
› Tel.: 06 5894333 - www.osteriafernanda.com
› Closed: Saturdays at lunch and Sundays
› Average price (excluding drinks): Euro 35,00

The Italian singer Claudio Baglioni sang a song that asked "What more could you have than Porta Portese" and the answer is: a meal at Osteria Fernanda. A welcoming and informal environment, Fernanda is based on Roman and Mediterranean cuisine offering classic dishes and reinterpretations of old classics that are always delicate and simple. The bread, the pasta and the desserts are all absolutely homemade.
Specialties: cacio e pepe-style pasta, gricia-style pasta

30|31

MASSENZIO

› Largo Corrado Ricci, 2-6 (Imperial Forum)
› Tel.: 06 6790706 - ristorantemassenzio@tiscali.it
  www.massenzioaifori.it
› Closed: Wednesdays
› Average price (excluding drinks): Euro 35,00

The adjacent Trajan's Market and the Imperial Forum are recreated stylishly inside "Massenzio" restaurant which offers its customers a vast external garden as well as an interior hall for dining. The menu faithfully follows Roman and Lazio gastronomic traditions without renouncing seafood, which is its specialty. The establishment has a self-service bar at lunch and they also have good pizza.
Specialties: amatriciana-style pasta, codfish, bruschetta, artichokes, crostini, "saltimbocca" veal slices, "supplì" rice croquettes

Spaghetti aglio, olio e peperoncino

Spaghetti with garlic, oil and hot pepper

› 400 g of spaghetti;
› 4 garlic cloves (peeled and crushed);
› hot pepper, extra virgin olive oil and salt to taste.

 QUICK   EASY

› ROMAN FORUM

THE HISTORY OF THE DISH

This very simple dish is always a hit.
Even when the refrigerator is empty, you
can always make it due to the simplicity
of the ingredients. It is important to use
good quality pasta and olive oil.

DIRECTIONS

While the water for the spaghetti is
heating, sauté the garlic in a pan with a
little oil and salt until the garlic starts
turning golden brown (be careful not to
burn it). Add the hot pepper, stir and
turn off the stove. Cook the spaghetti very
al dente, drain and pour it into the pan
with the garlic, oil and hot pepper and
cook on a high flame mixing quickly. Add
a touch of olive oil before serving. You
can also garnish it with a little parsley to
make the dish more colourful.

> THE CLOCK OF PIAZZA DI SIENA IN VILLA BORGHESE PARK

TRADITIONAL RESTAURANTS

MANCOS

> Via Sicilia, 150 (Villa Borghese Park)
> Tel.: 06 45422888
  steakhousemancos.altervista.org
  info@steakhousemancos.it
> Closed: Saturdays at lunch and Sundays
> Average price (excluding drinks): Euro 35,00

Mancos Restaurant is a truly young restaurant in every way: it opened in 2006 and it is managed by a young, dynamic and cordial staff. Fresh seafood, Argentine, Danish and Italian beef, a wine cellar with the best labels and good Mediterranean cuisine make Marcos an ideal restaurant for lunch or dinner, and it is just steps away from the green oasis of Villa Borghese Park.
Specialties: amatriciana-style pasta, cacio e pepe-style pasta, gricia-style pasta

Spaghetti all'Arrabbiata

Hot spicy spaghetti

> 400 g of spaghetti pasta;
> 500 g of tomato chunks or fresh peeled and deseeded tomato chunks;
> 3 garlic cloves (skinned and crushed);
> extra virgin olive oil, hot pepper and salt to taste;
> you can also add grated pecorino romano cheese and parsley.

 QUICK   EASY

THE HISTORY OF THE DISH

This is not a truly ancient dish, but due to its simplicity and delightful flavour, it has become popular quickly and has been well-known for some time. It is frequently served to friends as an impromptu late night snack. Many variations have been created from this basic recipe over the years: try adding bacon, mushrooms, black olives or vary it as you like.

DIRECTIONS

Fill a pan with salted water and boil. In the meantime sauté the garlic cloves and hot pepper. The moment the garlic begins to turn golden brown, add the tomatoes and salt and let it cook over a high flame. Cook the pasta al dente and top it with the sauce. For a more intense flavour you can drain the pasta a minute before it is ready and finish cooking it in the sauce. If you prefer, you can make your own creative variations by topping it with diced parsley and/or grated pecorino cheese.

Spaghetti
alla Carbonara

Spaghetti Carbonara

› 400 g of spaghetti pasta;
› 1 egg and 2 egg yolks;
› 120 g of pork jowl or unsmoked bacon cut into chunks;
› 150 g of grated pecorino romano cheese;
› extra virgin olive oil, salt and pepper to taste.

 QUICK   EASY

THE HISTORY OF THE DISH

Traditionally rigatoni pasta is used but the recipe is also great with spaghetti or bucatini. In Italian a "carbonara" is a charcoal maker, and this dish owes its name to the men who worked at the charcoal pits in the forests that once surrounded the city. The ease of the dish, the use of ingredients that are easy to conserve and the heartiness of this dish fit perfectly in that scenario.

DIRECTIONS

Heat a large pan with water and salt to cook the pasta. In the meantime beat the egg yolks together with the pecorino cheese and a generous serving of pepper. Sauté the pork in a large pan with a little oil until the fat has become transparent and the meat is crispy. Cook the pasta al dente, drain and place it in the pan to cook for a couple of minutes at a high flame. Remove it from the stove, add the beaten eggs and mix quickly. Serve it with other grated cheese to be added at pleasure. There are different schools of thought on this dish: many people add a finely diced onion to the pork while others prefer garlic, and still others use both: you decide.

RECOMMENDED WINE

BIANCO CAPENA (DOC)
This wine is produced in vineyards near the gates of Rome, around Capena on the western bank of the Tiber. The area has an ancient wine producing tradition, in fact Horace, Virgil and Cicero sang the praises of these prosperous vineyards. It is said that the wine of Capena was called "bianco Feronia" because it was offered to the nymph Feronia during sacrificial rites. It is a perfect dinner wine that is excellent with spaghetti alla carbonara or pasta all'amatriciana, seafood or freshwater fish, fried artichokes, zucchini, eggplant and omelettes.

TRADITIONAL RESTAURANTS

OSTERIA DEL SOSTEGNO

› Via delle Colonnelle, 5 (Piazza Colonna)
› Tel.: 06 6793842 – ilsostegno@hotmail.it
  www.ilsostegno.it
› Closed: Mondays
› Average price (excluding drinks): Euro 50,00

At the end of a quiet dead end street without cars, just steps away from the Pantheon and Piazza Colonna you will find Osteria del Sostegno. Sostegno means "support" in Italian and the establishment takes its name from the large metal support that sustains the building. The restaurant is small (there are few tables inside and outside) but comfortable. The wine list includes around sixty labels and the menu is filled with typical Roman specialties.
Specialties: amatriciana-style pasta, cacio e pepe-style pasta, carbonara-style pasta, "saltimbocca" veal slices

Spaghetti alla Gricia

Gricia-style spaghetti

 QUICK   EASY

› 400 g of spaghetti or bucatini;
› 150-200 g of pork jowl cut into pieces;
› 150 g of grated pecorino romano cheese;
› extra virgin olive oil, salt and pepper to taste.

THE HISTORY OF THE DISH

This recipe is similar to the more well known "amatriciana" style pasta, except it is made without tomato sauce. It originated in Grisciano, a town in the Upper Sabine area just a few kilometres from Amatrice: in fact originally the dish was known as "griscia". Still today the town hosts the Gricia Festival every August in honour of this simple yet tasty dish.

DIRECTIONS

Sauté the pork jowls in a non-stick pan with just a drop of oil and let them brown over a low flame until the fat becomes transparent. At your pleasure you can add 1/2 glass of dry white wine and allow it to evaporate at a high flame. Cook the spaghetti al dente and before draining add a ladle full of the pasta water to the sautéed mixture. Add the drained pasta and cook at a high flame for a few minutes. Stir continuously and add grated pecorino cheese. Serve piping hot while the cheese is still melted and top with fresh ground pepper.

› DOME - PANTHEON

LA SAGRESTIA

› Via del Seminario, 89 (Pantheon)
› Tel.: 06 6797581
› Closed: Wednesdays
› Average price (excluding drinks): Euro 20,00

La Sagrestia is a restaurant-pizzeria with a long-standing tradition located in a building from the fourteen hundreds very near the Pantheon. The restaurant serves Roman specialties as well as around twenty kinds of pizza.
Specialties: amatriciana-style pasta, cacio e pepe-style pasta, carbonara-style pasta, gricia-style pasta

Spaghetti cacio e pepe

Cheese and pepper pasta

› 400 g of spaghetti or vermicelli pasta;
› 150 g of fresh-grated pecorino cheese;
› lots of fresh ground pepper;
› salt to taste.

QUICK   EASY

THE HISTORY OF THE DISH

This is a "quick" first course that is great for unscheduled meals. The singularity of pecorino romano cheese makes the recipe great.

DIRECTIONS

Cook the spaghetti al dente and set aside a dish of the cooking water before draining the pasta. Drain the pasta (not completely) and place it in a warm dish. Add the pecorino cheese and pepper and mix quickly until the cheese melts, and add some of the pasta water you set aside if the mixture becomes too dry. Another even easier version calls for mixing the pecorino cheese and pepper with the water set aside from cooking the pasta, stirring quickly to melt the cheese and then pouring it over the pasta and mixing before serving.

RECOMMENDED WINE

TARQUINIA (DOC)
This production area involves the lands of various municipalities located between the provinces of Rome and Viterbo along the coastal strip that runs from Montalto di Castro to Fiumicino and, inland, from the Cimini mountains to the hills of Tolfa. The area has a mild climate with cool breezes that protect the vineyards from fungi and illnesses. The white is perfect with fish, and especially with oily fish, fried vegetables, soft cheese and omelettes. The red pairs well with flavourful first courses, grilled or roasted white and red meats. The rosé is a wine that is perfect for the whole meal and it pairs well with cold cuts, vegetable soups and somewhat mild cheeses.

Zuppa di fave con le cotiche

Fava beans and pork rind stew

› 800 g of dry fava beans;
› 300 g of fresh pork rind;
› 100 g of salt-cured ham (*prosciutto crudo*);
› 1 tablespoon of tomato sauce;
› 2 onions; parsley, marjoram, extra virgin olive oil, salt to taste and slices of toasted bread.

THE HISTORY OF THE DISH

This is a classic farm soup that is perfect for cold winter days. Made from humble ingredients or scrap cuts, this is a tasty and highly nutritious soup.

DIRECTIONS

Let the dry fava beans soak in water for at least two days. Drain them and place in a pan covered with water and then add salt and cook until they have become very soft (but not until they fall apart). Scrape and rinse the pork rind and allow it to boil for a few minutes. Then wash it again and cut the rind into pieces around three centimetres in size. Prepare a pesto made from finely chopped ham, parsley and marjoram and place it in a pot with a dash of oil. Let it heat and then add the diced onion. When the onion is golden brown, add a spoonful of tomato sauce. Allow the mixture to cook and season, then add the pork skins and some water and cook until the pork skins are done. Drain the fava beans, add them to the pot and cook the mixture together at a moderate heat for around fifteen minutes. Place a piece of lightly toasted bread in each bowl, pour the steaming hot soup over it and serve.

SECOND COURSES

The most characteristic Roman dishes give an idea of "the way Rome was".

The pastoral countryside, subject of so many paintings from the nineteenth-century, is still alive in the rooted tradition of suckling lamb, which is prepared in many different ways (a typical holiday treat). Roman cuisine reflects the vivacity and colour of Testaccio, the home of Rome's market and the historic slaughterhouse, which gave rise to the widespread use of the famous "fifth quarter": the less esteemed meats were destined to the tables of the commoners, who put them to good use considering that these dishes are still favourites.

The seafood cuisine is not as plentiful, but it should not be forgotten that once Rome was separated from the sea by forests and swamps, which somewhat slowed the development of seafood dishes. However, the seafood dishes that top traditional menus are appreciated for their flavour and creativity - reinterpreting the characteristics of Roman cuisine in a mariner's key.

TRADITIONAL RESTAURANTS

FELICE

› Via Mastro Giorgio, 29 (Testaccio)
› Tel.: 06 5746800 - info@feliceatestaccio.com
www.feliceatestaccio.com
› Closed: Sundays
› Average price (excluding drinks): Euro 40,00

The restaurant Felice is located in Testaccio (the most Roman neighbourhood of Rome) near the Garden of Oranges, which is definitely worthy a visit for the splendid panorama.
As tradition commands, the menu changes daily and it is read aloud by the waiter. Following Roman culinary traditions gnocchi are served on Thursdays, codfish is served on Fridays and tripe is served on Saturdays).
Specialties: lamb, amatriciana-style pasta, carbonara-style pasta, gricia-style pasta, roulade, tripe

Abbacchio brodettato

Lamb in broth

› 1 kg of lean lamb cut into pieces;
› 1 slice of salt-cured ham (*prosciutto crudo*) cut into chunks (50 g);
› 1 rounded tablespoon of flour;
› 1 diced onion;
› 1 glass of dry white wine;
› 2 garlic cloves (skinned and minced);
› 3 egg yolks;
› 1/2 a lemon;
› if you like, you can also add 2 tablespoons of parmesan or grana padana cheese;
› grated parsley, marjoram, extra virgin olive oil and salt and pepper to taste.

 TIME CONSUMING   DIFFICULT

THE HISTORY OF THE DISH

This dish is elaborate, sumptuous and original, and it makes for a smashing success. It was in fact and still is usually a traditional Easter lunch dish.

DIRECTIONS

In a deep pan with a heavy bottom slowly sauté the onion and lamb in olive oil. When the meat starts to brown, add salt, pepper and wine and cook until the liquid has evaporated. Cover the mixture with warm water and cook over a low flame in a covered pan. As soon as the liquid starts to boil remove one cup and mix the flour into it (take care not to form lumps). Pour the flour mixture back into the pan and cook for around twenty minutes or until the sauce becomes creamy. An easier version calls for breading the lamb in flour before browning it, but the result is slightly different. In the meantime beat the egg together with the parmesan cheese (to taste) and the lemon juice. At the end pour the garlic and parsley in the pan, mix it for a minute and remove the pan from the stove. Then slowly mix in the beaten egg allowing it to cook in the heat of the pan. Serve hot.

RECOMMENDED WINE

NETTUNO (DOC)
In the Nettuno countryside Cacchione grapes found their ideal habitat centuries ago.
This splendid local white grape grows in lands that are rich in silicon such as this area. Its uniqueness and characteristics have allowed for the continued production of the wine over the centuries.
This grape is used to make Nettuno, which has been a DOC wine since May 2003. The white pairs perfectly with molluscs and crustaceans, seafood salads, casseroles, soups, lasagne, stewed cuttlefish, cod, caciocavallo cheese and provola cheese. The red is well suited for more structured meals: baked white meats, roasted lamb and potatoes, medium aged cheeses. The Rosé is perfect for cold cut appetizers, vegetables minestrone and soups.

Abbacchio scottadito

Crispy lamb ribs

› 1 kg of lamb ribs;
› extra virgin olive oil, salt and pepper to taste.

 QUICK  EASY

THE HISTORY OF THE DISH

The excellence of simplicity: the success of this dish is all in the quality of the lamb (in Rome, suckling lamb is generally used). In Italian "scottadito" means 'burn your finger' because these tasty ribs are irresistible to eat with your fingers the moment they are removed from the flame ... which inevitably leads to the proverbial burnt finger.

DIRECTIONS

Flatten the ribs with a meat mallet, brush them with oil on both sides and add salt and pepper. If you like herbs you can also add a little tarragon. Cook them on a grill over a high flame (preferably over a charcoal fire) until they are crispy. You can also cook them on a very hot griddle for about 4 minutes per side. Serve with wedges of lemon as soon as they are ready.

RECOMMENDED WINE

CESANESE DI AFFILE OR AFFILE (DOC)
It is produced in the Roman hinterland, within the municipalities of Affile and Roiate and in the high Arcinazzo plains (around 600 meters above sea level). Cesanese di Affile wine derives almost completely from a grape with the same name, which is a local variety of the common Cesanese grape that is blended together with it in small quantities. It pairs well with flavourful dishes and spicy traditional cuisine, first courses with meat sauces, red meats and pork, rabbit and roasted lamb, pork ribs and pork chops, game, sharp cheeses and cold cuts. The dolce and spumante versions are great with desserts.

› CHURCH OF SAINT YVES AT LA SAPIENZA

TRADITIONAL RESTAURANTS

ANTICA TRATTORIA POLESE

› Piazza Sforza Cesarini, 40 (Corso Rinascimento)
› Tel.: 06 6861709 - www.trattoriapolese.it
  ristorantepolese@fastwebnet.it
› Closed: Tuesdays
› Average price (excluding drinks): Euro 30,00

Antica Trattoria Polese is located near the church of Saint Yves at La Sapienza (one of the masterpieces of Baroque architecture), just a few metres from Piazza Navona in a building from the fourteen hundreds, former residence of the Borgia family.
This pleasant trattoria has a relaxed and easy going environment and it is a point of reference for all those who love great Roman cuisine.
Specialities: lamb, amatriciana-style pasta, cacio e pepe-style pasta, carbonara-style pasta, Jewish-style artichokes, gricia-style pasta, ricotta cake

› THE THEATRE OF MARCELLUS

TRADITIONAL RESTAURANTS

BA" GHETTO

› Via del Portico d'Ottavia, 57 (Theatre of Marcellus)
› Tel.: 06 68892868 - info@kosherinrome.com - www.kosherinrome.com
› Closed: Friday evenings and Saturdays at lunch
› Average price (excluding drinks): Euro 30,00

> *Centuries of Jewish-Roman culinary traditions triumph at Ba" Ghetto, which is an elegant and cordial establishment located near the Theatre of Marcellus and Capitoline hill.*
> *The stairs lead inside the restaurant which is furnished in a simple manner with the kitchen at the back and tables covered in white tablecloths. The friendly and polite service provides a homey atmosphere.*
> *The menu includes Roman specialties prepared kosher.*
> *Specialities: anchovies with endive, codfish, carbonara-style pasta, Jewish-style artichokes*

Aliciotti con l'indivia

Anchovies with endive

⏰	MEDIUM
🍴	EASY

› 1 kg of fresh anchovies that have been cleaned and filleted;
› 1 kg of endive;
› extra virgin olive oil and salt to taste.

THE HISTORY OF THE DISH

This is another truly magnificent dish from Rome's Jewish community. It is delicious served warm, but it is also great served cold.

DIRECTIONS

Rinse the anchovies, cover them with salt and set them in a strainer to drain. Repeat this process with the endive: remove the core and exterior leaves, wash, chop, salt it and allow it to drain in a strainer. After a couple of hours prepare a baking dish with a little olive oil. Place a layer of endive in the dish covered by a layer of anchovies (continue layering the ingredients with endive as the top layer). If you like, you can also place tiny slivers of garlic in each layer. Cover it with olive oil and cook in the oven at 180° for around 45 minutes: after cooking there should be no water in the pan and the vegetables should be golden brown and crispy.

RECOMMENDED WINE

FRASCATI (DOC)
This is one of the oldest DOC wines and it has been recognised as a special typical product since 1933. Frascati is produced in the Castelli Romani hills in the municipalitiy of Frascati and the surrounding towns. The lands are of volcanic origin and they are rich in potassium, phosphorus and microelements which are permeable and dry. It is one of the oldest wine varieties and it filled the tables of ancient Romans back in the era of Tusculum's maximum splendour. It was made famous by Pope Paul III who used it at papal lunches. Exclusively white, it is produced in various varieties, which include the famous but rare Cannellino. It pairs well with appetizers, first or second courses of white meat or fish dishes, artichokes, omelettes, fried oily fish, vegetables and egg dishes. The dolce version is great to end a meal together with shortbread cookies or homemade desserts. The Cannellino variety pairs well with desserts like ricotta cake and the classic maritozzi.

KOSHER CUISINE

In Judaism eating is a sacred act and food preparation is regulated by a strict code of laws known as the kashrut.
Food must be kosher that is conforming to the laws of the Torah.
Impure animals are prohibited. The only animals allowed are ruminants with cloven hooves and therefore horses, pigs and animals such as hare, rabbit and camel are not allowed. All seafood is required to have fins and scales and therefore molluscs and crustaceans are not permitted.
Pure animals must be slaughtered by cutting the jugular vein to assure the complete removal of the blood and the meat is soaked under salt to remove any remaining traces. Not all of the animal parts may be eaten: the muscles and the bones are allowed, while the kidneys and the intestine are not.
In Kosher cuisine, meats and dairy products are not eaten at the same meal and even the pots and pans used to cook them are separate. Due to the prohibition of cooking meat and dairy together, cheeses that use animal-based rennet are not allowed. Furthermore, cheeses which have mold or microorganisms are not allowed, even if they are invisible, such as gorgonzola.
All fermented drinks are prohibited with the exception of wine, which must not contain prohibited ingredients or any sort of leavening, and it must be processed exclusively by observant Jews.

› EMELYN STORY - GRAVE IN THE PROTESTANT CEMETERY

TRADITIONAL RESTAURANTS

FLAVIO AL VELAVEVODETTO

› Via di Monte Testaccio 97-98 (Porta San Paolo)
› Tel.: 06 5744194
www.flavioalvelavevodetto.com
› Closed: Always open
› Average price (excluding drinks): Euro 30,00

The restaurant interior, which is inside the grottoes of Monte Testaccio, the panoramic terrace and the external courtyard are the unique characteristics that distinguish "Flavio al Velavevodetto". The cuisine of this restaurant, located in the heart of Testaccio near the Porta San Paolo gate and the Protestant Cemetery, is based on simplicity and the bounty of traditional Roman specialties.
Specialties: lamb, codfish, "coratella", gnocchi

Baccalà alla Trasteverina

Trastevere-style codfish

> › 800-1000 g of dried codfish (rehydrated and rinsed);
> › 200 g of flour; 2 onions; 2 anchovy fillets (rinsed);
> › 1 garlic clove; 1 spoonful of capers;
> › 40 g of raisins (softened in warm water);
> › 40 g of pine nuts; 1 lemon;
> › parsley, extra virgin olive oil and salt to taste.

 MEDIUM   AVERAGE

THE HISTORY OF THE DISH

Roman cuisine is all about intense and appetizing flavours, which are varied and well balanced. This decidedly tasty codfish is a fine example.

DIRECTIONS

Place the capers and raisins in water to soak. Rinse and drain the codfish then cut it into rectangular pieces (around 3 x 6 cm) and bread them in flour. Cook the codfish in a large pan with olive oil. When the codfish is golden brown on both sides, drain it and keep it warm. Sauté the garlic and the onion (chopped finely) in the drippings until they are golden brown: they should be cooked slowly. Add a little salt, cover the pan and cook over a low flame. After a couple of minutes add the drained capers, raisins and the pine nuts. Continue stirring for a minute and then turn the stove off. Add the diced anchovies and mix them into the rest of the mixture using a wooden spoon to crush them. Heat the oven to 220°, oil a baking pan and pour the cooked mixture into it. Then place the codfish over the top and cover it with a few teaspoons of olive oil from the sauce. After 5 minutes remove the pan from the stove, add the grated parsley and the lemon juice and serve.

RECOMMENDED WINE

COLLI DELLA SABINA (DOC)

This wine is produced in the Sabina hills, an ancient land that includes the areas between the province of Rome and Rieti, in a zone that has maintained its environmental integrity. The red wines should be paired with first courses with meat sauces, mushrooms, red meats, game and aged cheeses. The whites are suited to fish dishes (both fresh water and saltwater) vegetable minestrone, omelettes and mild cheeses. The rosé is perfect for dining and it is generally paired with cold cuts, risotto, fish or egg based dishes. The spumante versions are best as aperitifs or after dinner.

Bollito alla Picchiapò

"Picchiapò" simmered meats

› 700 g of boiled meats (veal or mixed meats);
› 2-3 red or yellow onions;
› 400-500 g of tomato chunks or tomato sauce;
› spice to taste with rosemary, basil, cinnamon, hot pepper, cloves and bay leaves;
› dry white or red wine, extra virgin olive oil and salt to taste.

THE HISTORY OF THE DISH

This dish was made famous by a scene from a movie entitled "We all loved each other so much" by Ettore Scola. This is a classic leftovers remake. The wisdom and creativity of the locals turned boiled meat leftovers into a fabulous specialty.

DIRECTIONS

Cut the boiled meat into bite size pieces. Cut the onion into thin slices and let it sauté in a large pan with oil. As soon as the onion begins to turn golden brown, add the wine and let it evaporate over a low flame. When the sauce in the pan has thickened add the tomato and the spices, salt to taste and let it simmer slowly. After around 10 minutes add the meat and continue cooking until the sauce has thickened.

RECOMMENDED WINE

VIGNANELLO (DOC)
Produced in the Vignanello area east of Viterbo on the slopes of the Cimini Hills over the Tiber valley; wine production in the area dates back to ancient times. The name itself, which recalls the term 'vigna' (grapevine), speaks of the important role it had in the local economy. The red pairs well with meat and vegetable appetizers, flavourful first courses, stuffed pasta, structured red meats, boiled meats, roasts, game, aged cheeses and grilled meat. The rosé is perfect with appetizers, cold cuts, omelettes and vegetables. The white pairs well with risotto and all sorts of fish based dishes. The Greco variety makes a lovely aperitif and it pairs well with molluscs, crustaceans and seafood.

› SAN PIETRO IN VINCOLI

TRADITIONAL RESTAURANTS

TRATTORIA MORGANA

› Via Mecenate, 19/21 (Rione Monti)
› Tel.: 06 4873122 - info@trattoriamorgana.com
  www.trattoriamorgana.com
› Closed: Sundays at dinner and Mondays
› Average price (excluding drinks): Euro 25,00

Trattoria Morgana is very close to Teatro Brancaccio and it is about 10 minutes from the church of San Pietro in Vincoli (where you can see the famous Moses by Michelangelo). The restaurant has a family style environment that is polite and upbeat. The restaurant serves typical Roman traditional cuisine (there are also some vegetarian specialties) and the desserts are all homemade.
Specialties: picchiapò-style simmered meats, gricia-style pasta, pasta and chickpeas, "puntarelle" chicory salad

Coda alla vaccinara

Italian oxtail stew

> › 1,5 kg of oxtail (beef or veal);
> › 100 g of fatback or pork jowl;
> › 1 carrot;
> › 1 onion;
> › 1 tender celery heart (remove the outer stalks);
> › 1 kg of tomato chunks;
> › 1 garlic clove;
> › 1 glass of dry white wine;
> › grated parsley, salt, pepper and extra virgin olive oil to taste.

THE HISTORY OF THE DISH

This is another example of the Roman talent for creative cooking ideas: scrap cuts give rise to yet another delightful dish. This recipe is named for the "vaccinari", who were the butchers at the historic Testaccio slaughterhouse. They were paid in part with the tails of the animals they slaughtered.

› FOUNTAIN OF THE FOUR RIVERS - PIAZZA NAVONA

DIRECTIONS

Cut the tail into 3-4 cm pieces. Rinse it and cook for 10 minutes in salted boiling water (double the time if you use beef tail). In the meantime crush together the fatback, parsley, garlic, onion and carrot. Brown the diced mixture in a large pan with a little olive oil until it starts to become golden brown, then add the meat. Let the mixture cook at a low flame and then add the wine, salt and pepper and continue cooking. When the wine has evaporated add the tomato, check the salt, cover and let it cook at a very low temperature, mixing occasionally and adding hot water as needed until the meat is tender and falls from the bone (this takes quite a while). Cut the celery into pieces, pour it into the pan and let it cook for another half an hour. Serve the oxtail stew piping hot covered with the flavourful sauce. There are also some common variations to this classic recipe. Some people add the celery to the crushed mixture at the beginning; others add 1 clove and hot pepper. If you like aromatic dishes, you can try adding cinnamon, nutmeg and marjoram during the last few moments of cooking.

TRADITIONAL RESTAURANTS

LA CAMPANA

› Vicolo della Campana, 18 (Piazza Navona)
› Tel.: 06 6875273
  www.ristorantelacampana.com
› Closed: Mondays
› Average price (excluding drinks): Euro 35,00

La Campana is the oldest restaurant in Rome that is still in business. The atmosphere is reminiscent of Rome in the 50s: it is a family-run restaurant-trattoria, the waiters are all locals and the atmosphere is uncomplicated. The menu contains all of the classics of Roman cuisine (and it has vegetarian selections as well as gluten free choices). It is located very near Piazza Navona and Piazza Sant'Eustachio in the heart of the Eternal City. Specialties: lamb, amatriciana-style pasta, codfish, carbonara-style pasta, artichokes, oxtail stew, zucchini flowers, chicken with bell peppers, "saltimbocca" veal slices, tripe

Coratella di abbacchio con i carciofi

Lamb offal and artichokes

› the heart, lungs and liver of a nursing lamb;
› 4 cleaned artichokes;
› 1 lemon;
› 1 glass of white wine;
› extra virgin olive oil, salt and pepper to taste.

 MEDIUM   EASY

THE HISTORY OF THE DISH

This is another very traditional dish which highlights poorer cuts of meat to make a fabulous recipe, as is characteristic of traditional cuisine.

DIRECTIONS

Cut the artichokes into thin slices and brown them on low heat with oil, salt, pepper and the juice of half a lemon. Cut the pieces of meat, separating the heart, lung and liver.
Due to the fact that the organs have different cooking times and methods, it is important to cook them separately. Heat some oil in a pan and softly brown the lung for 2 minutes, then add the heart and continue cooking for 4-5 minutes, then add the liver and do not cook for over 2 minutes.
Add the artichokes, salt to taste and pour wine in the pan. Careful to continue stirring; cook until the wine has evaporated.

RECOMMENDED WINE

COLLI ALBANI (DOC)
The territory of this DOC wine occupies the southern end of the Castelli Romani, which are the hills on the western banks of Albano Lake. The area has been known for its white wines for centuries. It is said that Colli Albani is the father of Castelli Romani wines and it should correspond with the ancient "Albano", a white wine which was well known in the days of the Roman empire. Here they were making wine even before Imperial times: it seems that the Latin community in Albalonga celebrated Jupiter Laterius by sacrificing "golden wine" to him. It is perfect with any fish or vegetable based dish and it is ideal with the traditional local cuisine including: cured meats and the famous roasted suckling pig of Ariccia, lamb cacciatore,"coratella" lamb offal, grilled pork livers, tripe stew and poultry dishes.

TRADITIONAL RESTAURANTS

RAGNO D'ORO

› Via Silla, 26
(Castel Sant'Angelo)
› Tel.: 06 3212362
www.ragnodoro.org
info@ragnodoro.org
› Closed: Mondays at lunch and Sundays
› Average price (excluding drinks): Euro 30,00

The trattoria-pizzeria "Da Marco e Fabio" (better known as "Ragno d'Oro") has been serving up cuisine based on authentic and wholesome flavours for over fifty years. This family run business has a rustic environment, a small exterior summer dining area, great food and a touch of Romanesque humour, which make this establishment located near Castel Sant'Angelo one of a kind. Specialities: lamb, amatriciana-style pasta, bruschetta, cacio e pepe-style pasta, carbonara-style pasta, Jewish-style artichokes, oxtail stew, "coratella", zucchini flowers, gricia-style pasta, "supplì" rice croquettes, tripe

> WINGED FIGURE - ALTARE DELLA PATRIA
(ALTAR OF THE FATHERLAND)

TRADITIONAL RESTAURANTS

INROMA AL CAMPIDOGLIO

› Via dei Fienili, 56 (Campidoglio)
› Tel.: 06 69191024 - inroma@inroma.eu
  www.inroma.eu
› Closed: Always open
› Average price (excluding drinks): Euro 35,00

This historic Roman establishment is located in a magnificent position at the foot of Capitoline Hill facing the Forum and the Altar of the Fatherland. It has two large terraces that provide a splendid view of ancient Rome. Dedicated almost entirely to cinema, it is much loved by artists and it has served as a set to many movies. The paintings on the walls are reminiscent of the days of the Dolce Vita.
The strong points are the homemade pasta and the great choice of wines.
Specialties: lamb, amatriciana-style pasta, codfish, cacio e pepe-style pasta, carbonara-style pasta, artichokes, "saltimbocca" veal slices

Filetti di baccalà in pastella

Fried codfish fillets

› 600 g of dried salted codfish (which has been rehydrated);
› 2 egg whites;
› 100 g of flour;
› extra virgin olive oil and salt to taste.

 MEDIUM   EASY

THE HISTORY OF THE DISH

This is a very traditional recipe and this fragrant dish of codfish is always part of the large fried foods platter that is customarily served on Christmas Eve.

DIRECTIONS

Mix the flour, one cup of cold water, very little salt and 2 tablespoons of oil. Set the batter aside. Cut the fish into narrow fillets around 15 centimetres long. Beat the egg white into a meringue and add it to the batter. Then dip the fillets into the batter and deep fry. When they are crispy on both sides, remove them and lay on paper towels to drain before serving. Serve with slices of lemon to squeeze onto the fillets.

RECOMMENDED WINE

MARINO (DOC)

This is possibly the strongest of the Castelli Romani wines. It is full bodied and intense. The wine is produced in a fairly small area in the lands surrounding the town of Marino and the nearby area on a strip of hills that face the Tyrrhenian coast. An ancient tradition takes place every year in celebration of this wine. During the town wine festival, the city's "Fountain of the Moors" is filled with wine instead of water. The full-bodied flavour of this wine pairs well with traditional Roman cuisine, such as fried cod fillets, risotto with asparagus or porcini mushrooms, fish based dishes, white meat cacciatore, omelettes, mild cold cuts and fresh cheeses. The amabile and dolce varieties are a great end to a meal.

IL MATRICIANO

› Via dei Gracchi, 55 (Piazza Risorgimento)
› Tel.: 06 32500364
› Closed: Wednesdays (Saturdays during summer months)
› Average price (excluding drinks): Euro 45,00

Right in the shade of "der Cuppolone", which is how Romans refer to the dome of St. Peter's, you will find Il Matriciano, one of the most famous restaurants in Rome where you can try traditional Roman specialties.
The restaurant offers good service and it is a well furnished and refined establishment. The environment is pleasant, relaxed and informal (outdoor dining is also possible). Due to its notoriety, the restaurant is frequently crowded, so reservations are recommended.
Specialties: lamb, amatriciana-style pasta, oxtail stew, fried foods, tripe

Fritto alla Romana
Fried foods platter

› 3 Romanesque artichokes (other varieties are also fine);
› 300 g of veal or lamb brains;
› 1 fresh mozzarella;
› 200 g of sheep milk ricotta (if you cannot find sheep milk ricotta locally, you can substitute it with cow milk ricotta mixed with finely grated pecorino romano cheese);
› 2 tart baking apples (grey pippins are commonly used if you can find them);
› 2-3 zucchini; 600 g of green cauliflower tips or cardoons;
› 3 eggs; 1 lemon;
› flour, nutmeg, vinegar, extra virgin olive oil and salt to taste.

 TIME CONSUMING   DIFFICULT

› THE DOME OF ST. PETER'S

THE HISTORY OF THE DISH

The Roman fried foods platter requires a great deal of patience and skill, but the results are truly amazing. The basic version calls for brains, sweetbreads (the thymus gland located in the neck of cows and sheep) and classic Romanesque artichokes. However, you can substitute freely depending on your needs or the seasons. The vegetarian version is frequently served as an appetizer and it is a standard specialty at the "meatless" meal served on Christmas Eve.

DIRECTIONS

Clean the artichokes and remove all of the tough outer leaves. Immediately place the artichokes in water and lemon juice to keep them from browning. Then cut the artichokes into wedges leaving only 2-3 cm of the leg. Wash the brains and sweetbreads, boil them for a moment in water with a little vinegar; allow them to dry, remove any loose membranes and cut them into cubes. Wash and cut the zucchini into strips; clean the broccoli or cardoons, and cut them into large chunks and cook for 2-3 minutes in boiling water. Place a beaten egg and a little salt in one dish and flour in another. Individually bread all of the pieces in flour and then in the egg. If you decide to also prepare the fried apple (cut in 1/2 cm thick wedges), you should add a little nutmeg to the batter and cover the slices with powdered sugar after frying. The ricotta and the mozzarella are the most delicate to fry. It is easier if you cut them into slices a few hours beforehand and allow them to drain in a strainer. For the cheeses you should use a light batter that has a little salt. Fill a pan with oil and when it is hot begin frying the pieces a few at a time. When the batter has turned golden brown, remove the pieces with a slotted spoon and place on paper towels to drain. Add salt as necessary. Serve piping hot with lemon wedges to use as a condiment.

Involtini sedano e carote

Celery and carrot meat rolls

 MEDIUM

AVERAGE

› 600 g of thin red veal slices;
› 1 glass of dry white wine;
› 500 g of tomato chunks;
› 100 g of salt-cured ham (*prosciutto crudo*) or unsmoked bacon cut into thin strips;
› 2 carrots; 2-3 stalks of celery;
› 1 onion; 1 garlic clove;
› parsley, basil, salt, pepper and extra virgin olive oil to taste.

THE HISTORY OF THE DISH

This tasty dish is even loved by those who are not meat enthusiasts thanks to its rich flavour. The sauce is also great over pasta.

DIRECTIONS

Clean 2 of the celery stalks and 1 of the carrots and cut them lengthwise into 4-5 cm sticks around 1/2 cm thick. Lay the meat and top each slice with salt, pepper, a little ham or bacon and diced garlic, parsley and/or basil (the latter are optional). At the

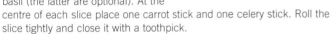

centre of each slice place one carrot stick and one celery stick. Roll the slice tightly and close it with a toothpick.
Dice the onion, the remaining celery stick and carrot and sauté them in a large pan with olive oil. Add the veal rolls, sauté them briefly on both sides and pour in the wine so that it sizzles.
Add the tomato, check the salt and let it continue cooking over a medium heat for at least 15 minutes. If the sauce becomes too thick add water. Remove the toothpicks and serve piping hot.

RECOMMENDED WINE

CIRCEO (DOC)
The production area extends along the southern coastal strip of Lazio in the National Circeo Park.
This area, like all of the Agro Pontino, has a unique history since it is made up of fertile lands that were never cultivated until the beginning of the 1900s.
After reclamation of the swamps in the area, the territory was cultivated with vineyards by the colonies that settled there and introduced wines such as Trebbiano, Sangiovese and Merlot. In recent times Circeo DOC has sought to expand its market by broadening the types of wine produced and by improving the quality.
The white wines are usually suited for pairing with oily fish, fried foods, buffalo or cow milk mozzarella and omelettes, while the rosé pairs well with soups, ricotta and cold cuts.
The reds are suited for full bodied dishes, roasted or grilled meats and aged cheeses.

TRADITIONAL RESTAURANTS

DAR CORDARO

› Piazzale Portuense, 4 (Porta Portese)
› Tel.: 06 5836751
› Closed: Mondays and Sundays
› Average price (excluding drinks): Euro 30,00

"Dar Cordaro", which is reminiscent of Rome in the 50s, is located near the Pontifical Arsenal inside a small house built in the arches of the Porta Portese gate.
The restaurant is managed by a Roman family that faithfully follows Roman culinary traditions. The environment inside is lively and well furnished and the service is friendly and easy going. Specialties: amatriciana-style pasta, cacio e pepe-style pasta, carbonara-style pasta, oxtail stew, gricia-style pasta, roulade, tripe

› FRUIT AND VEGETABLE STAND IN CAMPO DE' FIORI

TRADITIONAL RESTAURANTS

IL GRAPPOLO D'ORO

› P.zza della Cancelleria, 80/84 (Campo de' Fiori)
› Tel.: 06 6897080 - www.grappolodorozampano.it
  grappolodorozampano@virgilio.it
› Closed: Tuesdays and Wednesday at lunch
› Average price (excluding drinks): Euro 35,00

Grappolo d'Oro is located very near Campo de' Fiori in the heart of Rome. This historic restaurant of traditional Roman cuisine opened at the start of the 1900s.
The food is wonderful (fresh high quality ingredients, with homemade pasta and desserts), the service is impeccable and there is a good selection of wines.
Specialties: lamb, amatriciana-style pasta, codfish, cacio e pepe-style pasta, carbonara-style pasta, chicken with bell peppers

Pollo con i peperoni

Chicken with bell peppers

› 1 chicken (cleaned and cut into pieces);
› 2 yellow or red bell peppers;
› 50 g of ham cut into strips;
› 300 g of tomato chunks (or fresh juicy tomatoes);
› garlic, marjoram, white wine, extra virgin olive oil, salt and pepper to taste.

 MEDIUM   EASY

THE HISTORY OF THE DISH

This traditional dish has always been a hit. It was a typical speciality on weekends or summer holidays and it is a classic August 15th holiday dish.

DIRECTIONS

In a pan, sauté the ham in oil.
Add the chicken and brown all of the parts.
Then add salt, pepper, garlic, marjoram and the tomatoes.
Let the mixture cook for 10 minutes and then add the wine and let it continue cooking over a high flame.
Clean the peppers and cut them into small slices and roast them in a pan with salt, garlic and oil.
When the chicken is cooked, add the peppers and continue cooking to allow the flavours to mingle - and then serve.

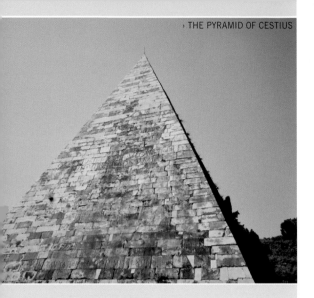

TRADITIONAL RESTAURANTS

DA ENZO

› Via Ostiense, 36/I (Piramide)
› Tel.: 06 5741364
› Closed: Sundays and Mondays at lunch
› Average price (excluding drinks): Euro 30,00

Not many people are aware that the Eternal City also has a pyramid (the Pyramid of Cestius), but it is worthwhile knowing that in the shade of the pyramid, you can find "Da Enzo" restaurant. This small establishment is decorated like diners of days gone by with white and red chequered tablecloths, an old-fashioned icebox, frescoes of Rome on the walls and a few tables outside for dining. "Da Enzo" is a traditional Roman neighbourhood trattoria where you can find traditional Roman dishes.
Specialities: amatriciana-style pasta, carbonara-style pasta, zucchini flowers, "saltimbocca" veal slices

Saltimbocca alla Romana

Roman-style veal slices

› 8 small slices of veal cut finely;
› 4 slices of salt-cured ham (*prosciutto crudo*);
› 8 leaves of sage;
› 1/2 glass of dry white wine;
› butter, flour, salt and pepper to taste.

 QUICK   EASY

THE HISTORY OF THE DISH

The aroma of sage adds a touch of class to this simple and much-loved recipe.

DIRECTIONS

Place a leaf of sage and 1/2 a slice of ham on each cut of veal, attaching them with a toothpick. Bread the meat in the flour. Melt the butter in a pan and grill the meat at a high flame on both sides. Then top it with salt and pepper in the areas without ham. Remove the pan from the stove and the meat from the pan, take out the toothpicks and keep warm. Put the pan back on the stove and add wine and more butter to the drippings. Cook until it makes gravy and then pour it boiling hot over the meat.

RECOMMENDED WINE

COLLI ETRUSCHI VITERBESI (DOC)
These DOC wines are produced in a vast area that includes 38 municipalities in the province of Viterbo up to the borders of Tuscany. It is an area that has been making wine since the times of the Etruscans. The zone extends across a hilly landscape with a mild climate thanks to the nearby Tyrrhenian Sea and Bolsena Lake along the banks of which the vineyards are planted. The wines include several white, red and rosé varieties.

Seppie
con carciofi

Cuttlefish and artichokes

› 700 g of cleaned cuttlefish;
› 4 cleaned artichokes (traditionally Romanesque artichokes are used, but others varieties work fine as well);
› 1 lemon;
› onion, garlic, parsley, extra virgin olive oil, salt and pepper to taste.

 MEDIUM   EASY

THE HISTORY OF THE DISH

Less famous than cuttlefish and peas, this combination is also based on the contrast between the delicate artichoke and the savoury cuttlefish - a grand match.

DIRECTIONS

Cut the artichokes into slices and put them in water and lemon juice (to keep them from darkening). Wash the cuttlefish and cut into strips. Sauté the oil, garlic and chopped onion, then add the artichokes well drained, salt and pepper and cook for around ten minutes adding water if necessary. Add the cuttlefish and one cup of hot water. Adjust the salt and pepper and continue cooking for around 15 minutes or until the broth has reduced into a gravy. Remove the pan from the flame and add chopped parsley, the juice of half a lemon and top with olive oil.

RECOMMENDED WINE

COLLI LANUVINI (DOC)
The production area is part of the Castelli Romani zone in the Genzano and Lanuvio area along the banks of the Lake of Nemi all the way to Aprilia. This wine was much praised by the ancient Roman writers and in the 1600s by the Baroque poet Metastasio. It is a white wine made from the classic grape varieties traditionally grown in the Castelli zone. It is retained as a wine that is suitable for the whole dinner, but it is best with first courses with vegetable sauces and freshwater fish, soups, fried fish, roasted or au gratin oily and freshwater fish, spicy white meats, eggs, asparagus and artichokes.

TRADITIONAL RESTAURANTS

DA LUCIA

› Vicolo del Mattonato, 2/B (Trastevere)
› Tel.: 06 5803601
› Closed: Mondays
› Average price (excluding drinks):
  Euro 30,00

"Da Lucia" trattoria can be found in the heart of historic Rome in the Trastevere district.
Managed by the same family for over 70 years, the helpings are generous as classic Roman tradition commands. The desserts are homemade and there are around thirty different wines available. In the summers there are tables outside for dining and enjoying the atmosphere of the tiny lanes of Trastevere to the fullest.
Specialities: lamb, amatriciana-style pasta, arrabbiata-style pasta, codfish, cacio e pepe-style pasta, gricia-style pasta, roulade, pasta and broccoli with rayfish, peas, cuttlefish, tripe

Spezzatino col sugo

Italian beef stew

 TIME CONSUMING

EASY

› 800 g of red veal cut into stew chunks;
› 1 onion; 1 carrot; 1 celery stalk;
› 1 garlic clove;
› 1 glass of dry white wine or meat broth;
› 400 g of tomato chunks;
› extra virgin olive oil, salt and pepper to taste.

THE HISTORY OF THE DISH

Beyond making a fine second course during the winter season, this tasty meat dish also makes a great topping: if you increase the quantity of tomato chunks, you can make a fabulous and hearty pasta sauce. You can also vary it by adding chunks of potatoes, peas or mushrooms during the last half hour of cooking time.

DIRECTIONS

In a large pan sauté the finely diced onion, carrot, celery and garlic in olive oil. After a couple of minutes add the meat and allow it to cook over a high flame for another 2 minutes, stirring. Pour in the tomato and add salt and pepper. Turn the stove down and let it simmer slowly in a covered pan. Stir and add wine (or broth) if necessary and continue cooking for at least 1 hour and half.

RECOMMENDED WINE

CESANESE DEL PIGLIO (DOC)
This wine is produced in the pre-Apennine zone of the Ciociaria area, near the municipality of Piglio, in the province of Frosinone. The grape, which is used almost purely, is Cesanese di Affile, a local variety of the more common Cesanese. It is ideal for accompanying foods from the Ciociaria zone, fettuccine with meat sauce, roasted or stewed meats, cold cuts and seasoned cheeses, lamb cacciatore, grilled pork livers, tripe and wild game. The amabile, dolce and spumante varieties pair well with cookies, desserts, cakes and fruit pies.

› FOUNTAIN OF THE FOUR RIVERS - PIAZZA NAVONA

TRADITIONAL RESTAURANTS

ALFREDO E ADA

› Via dei Banchi Nuovi, 14 (Piazza Navona)
› Tel.: 06 6878842
› Closed: Saturdays, Sundays
› Average price (excluding drinks): Euro 25,00

"Alfredo e Ada" is a classic trattoria just like they were in the old days (it opened over a century ago), and it is very near Piazza Navona. The small establishment has wooden tables and chairs, paper napkins, antique photographs on the walls, house wine and a traditional menu filled with homemade specialties. There are no appetizers and only one first course is served each day while you can choose between 3-4 second courses. There are no desserts or coffee to end your meal, but there are wonderful ciambelline cookies served with red wine, which can be followed up by a limoncello, a bitter or a grappa on the house. Specialities: amatriciana-style pasta, carbonara-style pasta, gricia-style pasta, "spezzatino" stew, tripe

Trippa alla Romana

Roman-style tripe

› 1 kg of cleaned tripe;
› 700 g of tomato chunks;
› 2 onions; 2 stalks of celery;
› 2 carrots;
› 150 g of grated pecorino romano cheese;
› 1 glass of dry white wine;
› fresh spearmint, cloves, basil, bay leaves, salt, pepper, hot pepper and extra virgin olive oil to taste.

TIME CONSUMING

EASY

THE HISTORY OF THE DISH

Tripe is part of the famous "fifth fourth": which is how they referred to the offal and scrap cuts of meat in Italy. It is a traditional dish that is frequently served on Saturdays, which was slaughter day in the past. The Roman style recipe has two essential ingredients, which are characteristic: the pecorino cheese and the spearmint are both very Roman; in fact spearmint is referred to as "menta romana" in Italian. It is important to use high quality tripe (the darker kind is the best). These days you can also find pre-boiled tripe which cuts down the preparation time.

DIRECTIONS

Boil the tripe for half an hour in salted water with half of the onions, celery, carrots and herbs and spices. Drain and cut into slices around 5 cm long and 2 cm wide. Sauté the remaining herbs and spices in a little oil (set aside a few mint leaves). After a couple of minutes add the tripe. Stir and add the glass of wine. When the wine has evaporated, add the tomato chunks, salt and pepper and cook in a covered pan at a low temperature, add water if necessary. At the end, add the remaining mint and allow it to cook for another minute. Serve hot covered with grated pecorino cheese.

The vegetables of the Roman countryside (and Lazio) are true specialties: artichokes, broccoli, fava beans, peas, fennel, salad tomatoes, zucchini and many other varieties of specific Romanesque breed vegetables are truly unique - enriching the local cuisine with excellent side dishes.

What can we say about the famous puntarelle? This plant is also sold in other areas as Catalogna chicory, but Rome "invented" a new way of using it: instead of cooking the leaves, as is customary with other greens, in Rome they are used as raw crunchy sprouts, which are cut with mastery so that they curl and then they are topped with an irresistible dressing. It is a truly original idea and an absolutely delicious side dish.

Another element that characterizes Roman side dishes are the tasty kosher specialties that can be found in the historic Jewish quarter and which have always adorned Roman tables.

› INSIDE THE BASILICA OF SAINT JOHN LATERAN

TRADITIONAL RESTAURANTS

DOMENICO DAL 1968

› Via Satrico, 23-25 (S. Giovanni)
› Tel.: 06 70494602 - info@domenicodal1968.it
  www.domenicodal1968.it
› Closed: Sundays and Mondays
› Average price (excluding drinks): Euro 40,00

Not far from St. John Lateran, the oldest church in Rome, you will find "Domenico dal 1968". This restaurant has a warm and friendly atmosphere, cordial and prompt service and it serves homemade Roman traditional cuisine.
Wines from Lazio are served.
Specialties: amatriciana-style pasta, carbonara-style pasta, Jewish-style artichokes, oxtail stew, gricia-style pasta

Carciofi alla "Giudia"

MEDIUM

EASY

Jewish style artichokes

› 6-8 cleaned Romanesque or Cimaroli artichokes (others varieties work fine as well);
› lots of extra virgin olive oil, salt and pepper to taste.

THE HISTORY OF THE DISH

This is the most famous dish of the Roman Jewish community. The recipe owes its success to its simplicity, which highlights the qualities of the artichoke to the utmost.

DIRECTIONS

Soak the artichokes in water and lemon for around ten minutes, drain and allow them to dry. Then beat the artichoke face down on a counter top to open the flower. Heat oil on a medium flame until it boils and then place the artichokes into the oil with the flower side down by holding them on the bottom of the pan with a fork until they are crispy. At this point, turn the artichokes upside down and let them cook until the heart is soft. Drain the artichokes and lay them on a paper towel to dry.
Top with salt and pepper: they are best served piping hot.

HOW DO YOU CLEAN ARTICHOKES?

Artichokes are frequently used in traditional Roman specialties.
How do you properly clean an artichoke?
Before beginning, it is better to rub your hands with lots of lemon juice. This helps keep them from staining and it will make them easier to clean.
If your artichoke is sold with the stem, remove any leaves which have thorns, detach the "head" of the artichoke (called the capolino), and throw away all of the stem except the most tender part (2-3 cm).
The outer leaves of the artichoke (called brattee) are hard and fibrous and they need to be removed. To do this, slip a knife under each leaf and pull it away from the stem until it detaches.
To reach the heart of the artichoke, you need to take off at least two or three layers until you reach the thinner and lighter coloured leaves. You also need to cut off the tip of the artichoke, which is the hardest part.
To prepare the stem of the artichoke, peel away the fibrous exterior leaving only the central core (which is lighter and tenderer).
After having cleaned the artichokes, they should be kept in water and lemon juice until you are ready to cook them.

Carciofi alla Romana

Roman style artichokes

MEDIUM   AVERAGE

› 8 well-cleaned Romanesque or Cimaroli artichokes (other varieties work fine as well)
› 2 cloves of garlic
› 1 bunch of mentuccia mint (if mentuccia mint is unavailable locally, use fresh mint)
› 3 or 4 pieces of parsley, 1 lemon, 1 glass of extra virgin olive oil
› salt and pepper to taste.

THE HISTORY OF THE DISH

This is a much loved homage to the artichoke, which has always grown magnificently in the Agro Romano area.

› SANTI QUATTRO INCORONATI BASILICA

TRADITIONAL RESTAURANTS

DA DANILO

› Via Petrarca, 13 (Via Merulana)
› Tel.: 06 77200111 - www.trattoriadadanilo.it
› Closed: Sundays
› Average price (excluding drinks): Euro 40,00

Photographs of celebrities line the walls of this warm and friendly establishment with courteous service and great cuisine that celebrates the best of Roman traditional specialties: "Da Danilo" is all this and much more. The establishment, which is located just a few minutes from the famous "Santi Quattro Incoronati" Basilica in the Esquiline district, makes one of the best versions of pasta alla carbonara served in the city.
Specialities: cacio e pepe-style pasta, carbonara-style pasta, artichokes

DIRECTIONS

Beat the artichoke face down on a counter top to delicately open the flower. Remove the small central leaves. Finely dice the tender parts of the artichoke stem, the garlic, the parsley and the mint. Top the diced mixture with a tablespoon of oil, salt and pepper and then fill the artichoke heart with the mixture and salt the outside as well. Place the artichokes face head down tightly packed in a ceramic dish that just barely contains them, top them with oil and add 6 tablespoons of water. Cover and let the artichokes cook at a medium flame for around 40 minutes. They should be tender and the water should have evaporated by the end of the cooking process. They are also great served cold or at room temperature.

RECOMMENDED WINE

ZAGAROLO (DOC)
This wine is produced in the hills between the Colli Albani and Colli Prenestini hills in the area of the town of Zagarolo and its surroundings. It is an area where the agricultural property is divided into small lots which creates evident limits on the production levels, and therefore it is produced in small quantities. It is a good wine for aperitifs and ideal for flavourful appetizers, Roman ricotta, buffalo mozzarella, pasta with seafood sauces, artichokes, omelettes, clam and mussel soup and fried seafood.

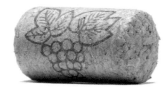

Concia
di zucchine

Pickled zucchini

⏰ TIME CONSUMING   👨‍🍳 EASY

› 1,5 kg of zucchini;
› 4 garlic cloves;
› white wine vinegar, extra virgin olive oil, basil and salt to taste.

THE HISTORY OF THE DISH

This is a traditional dish which originates in the Roman Jewish community. It is delicious and it keeps well in the refrigerator for several days. The original recipe calls for "romanesque" zucchini which are lighter in colour and star shaped, but if you have difficulty finding them locally you can also use other varieties of zucchini.

DIRECTIONS

Wash the zucchini and cut them lengthwise into thin strips. Place the slices in a single layer on a towel and let them dry for 24 hours (if the weather is nice, it is best to let them dry in the sun). In the meantime marinate the chopped basil and garlic in 1/2 glass of vinegar. When the zucchini are very dry, heat a large frying pan with a good deal of oil and fry the strips a few at a time. Let them drain on paper towels and then lay them in layers in a glass dish, salting between each layer. Pour the vinegar and herbs into the dish, cover and set aside. The next day, put the bottom layer of zucchini on the top and let it marinate for one day before using.
There are a few variations that also call for adding fresh mint, oregano, toasted pine nuts and topping it all with olive oil and vinegar.

RECOMMENDED WINE

ORVIETO (DOC)

The production area of this wine is located on the high hills along the banks of the Paglia river around the town of Orvieto, reaching to the upper Lazio territory. The local wine production dates back to very ancient times when the first inhabitants, the Etruscans, understood that the tuff rock, which made up these lands, was perfect for conserving wine. There are many documents and anecdotes that serve as testimony to the greatness of this wine from past centuries. The poet Gabriele D'Annunzio defined it as "bottled Italian sunshine" and Pope Gregory XVI ordered in his will that he be bathed in Orvieto wine before being buried. The Orvieto secco pairs nicely with fish, crustaceans and sea food or white meats, vegetables and fresh cheeses. The abbocato variety makes a nice aperitif or dessert wine.

TRADITIONAL RESTAURANTS

LA TAVERNA DEL GHETTO

› Via del Portico d'Ottavia, 8 (Ghetto)
› Tel.: 06 68809771
  www.latavernadelghetto.com
› Closed: Friday evenings
› Average price (excluding drinks): Euro 40,00

Very near the Synagogue in the heart of the old Roman Jewish quarter, you can find the Taverna del Ghetto where the oldest tradition of Jewish-Roman kosher cuisine remains intact. The welcoming environment is rustic and well maintained with an atmosphere of one of the most picturesque places of ancient Rome. Specialties: lamb, amatriciana-style pasta, codfish, carbonara-style pasta, Jewish-style artichokes, pickled zucchini, "coratella", gnocchi, "puntarelle" chicory salad

› PIAZZA DELLA SCALA IN TRASTEVERE

TRADITIONAL RESTAURANTS

DA AUGUSTO

› Piazza de Renzi, 15
› Tel.: 06 5803798
› Closed: Saturdays evenings and Sundays
› Averange price (excluding drinks): Euro 20,00

Specialties: amatriciana-style pasta, cod-fish, cacio e pepe-style pasta, carbonara-style pasta, artichokes, gnocchi, "puntarelle" chicory salad, "spezzatino" stew

Piselli al guanciale

Peas and pork

› 1,5 kg of fresh peas;
› 200 g of pork jowl;
› 1 small onion;
› 1 cup of vegetable broth;
› extra virgin olive oil, salt and pepper to taste.

 QUICK   EASY

THE HISTORY OF THE DISH

This is a great side dish and it is even better if you can find small fresh peas, which are sweeter and tenderer.

DIRECTIONS

Shell the peas and pour into a large pan after having sautéed the thinly sliced onion and pork jowl cubes in a little olive oil. Add salt and pepper and after a few minutes add a little of the broth. Let it cook for 10-15 minutes mixing well and adding broth if necessary. The pork jowl may be substituted with unsmoked bacon or salt-cured ham (*prosciutto crudo*). Peas cooked in this manner also make a great pasta topping, just add a little cream to help it blend more easily.

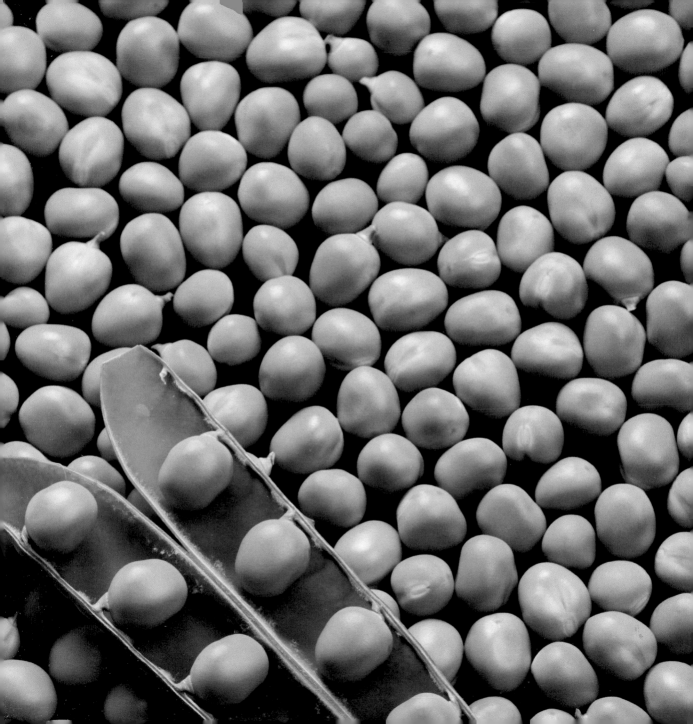

Puntarelle

Catalogna chicory shoots

- › 700 g of Catalogna chicory shoots: washed, cut and "curled";
- › 1 garlic clove;
- › 6 anchovies packed in oil;
- › vinegar, extra virgin olive oil and salt to taste.

DIRECTIONS

Drain the puntarelle and let them dry. Use a mortar and pestle to grind the garlic and anchovies into a creamy paste; then add vinegar and oil and mix. Dress the puntarelle with the mix and add salt to taste.

THE HISTORY OF THE DISH

This wintery side dish is always present at Christmas Eve dinners. Catalogna is a special variety of chicory that is crispy and bitter. The leaves are removed one by one, washed and cut from the bottom to the point at which the stem is hollow on the inside. Then cut the stems lengthwise into small thin strips and place them in very cold water for 30 minutes (ice water is even better). This makes the puntarelle curl and eliminates the bitterness.

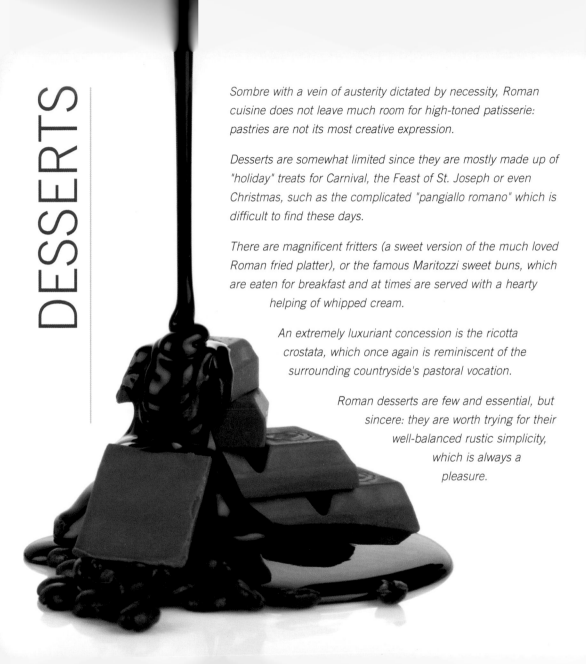

DESSERTS

Sombre with a vein of austerity dictated by necessity, Roman cuisine does not leave much room for high-toned patisserie: pastries are not its most creative expression.

Desserts are somewhat limited since they are mostly made up of "holiday" treats for Carnival, the Feast of St. Joseph or even Christmas, such as the complicated "pangiallo romano" which is difficult to find these days.

There are magnificent fritters (a sweet version of the much loved Roman fried platter), or the famous Maritozzi sweet buns, which are eaten for breakfast and at times are served with a hearty helping of whipped cream.

An extremely luxuriant concession is the ricotta crostata, which once again is reminiscent of the surrounding countryside's pastoral vocation.

Roman desserts are few and essential, but sincere: they are worth trying for their well-balanced rustic simplicity, which is always a pleasure.

Bignè di San Giuseppe

St. Joseph Beignets

 MEDIUM   AVERAGE

FOR THE BEIGNETS:
› 90 g of flour; 3 eggs; 40 g of butter;
› 100 g of vanilla sugar (if you cannot buy vanilla sugar locally, you can make it by mixing 1 teaspoon of vanilla extract with 200 g of sugar in the blender until it becomes powdered) plus 20 g of powdered sugar;
› lemon, extra virgin olive oil, shortening and salt to taste.

FOR THE CUSTARD CREAM:
› 4 level tablespoons of sugar;
› 2 heaping tablespoons of flour;
› 3 egg yolks;
› 1/2 litre of milk;
› lemon zest or vanilla sugar.

THE HISTORY OF THE DISH

This is a holiday treat: up until a few years ago, it was only eaten during the middle of March near the Feast of St. Joseph. Now these beignets have lost their holiday role and they can almost always be found, sometimes in interesting new variations.

DIRECTIONS

First of all prepare the custard cream. Add the egg yolks, the sugar and then the flour; slowly pour in the milk taking care not to form lumps. Then add lemon zest or vanilla. Cook in a pan on the stove and stir constantly in the same direction until it reaches a boil. Place the cream in the refrigerator and allow it to cool.

To prepare the beignets, mix the flour and the powdered sugar. In a pan heat 6 tablespoons of water, the butter and add a pinch of salt. After the butter has melted, turn off the flame and pour in all of the flour and sugar, mix the batter and place the mixture back onto the stove. Continue stirring and cook the mixture until it sizzles. Turn off the heat and pour it into a terrine: when it has cooled, add the eggs one at a time (two whole eggs and one egg yolk) and the lemon zest. Let the mixture sit for half an hour and then drop walnut-sized portions of the batter into hot oil and fry. When the beignets have raised and are golden, place them on paper towels to remove any excess oil.

Use a pastry bag or pastry filler to inject the filling into the beignets, then top with powdered sugar and serve.

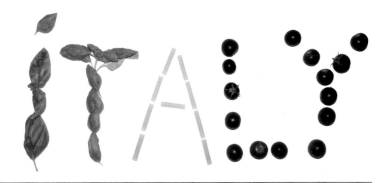

ROMAN CUISINE IN NEW YORK

"La Lupa", "Cacio e Pepe", "Testaccio", "Quinto Quarto" and "Sora Lella" are restaurants that all serve traditional roman cuisine. So what's the innovation? None of them are located in the Eternal City, but in the Big Apple. Roman cuisine has docked in New York and conquered America.

On the menus of these restaurants, which are continuing to expand (six were opened in 2010 alone) New Yorkers can find the following dishes: spaghetti in spicy tomato sauce (spaghetti all'arrabbiata), Jewish-style artichokes (carciofi alla Giudia), and lamb chops (agnello scottadito) or Roman veal slices (saltimbocca alla romana).

However New York is only the docking point for this new cuisine that is conquering the United States.

Aside from new restaurants specialized in "Roman cuisine", stores that sell the ingredients are also on the rise making it possible to find chicory for puntarelle, fresh pasta such as tonnarelli and tagliatelle, DOP pecorino romano cheese and DOP ricotta romana for making tasty Roman specialties, even on the other side of the Atlantic.

Castagnole

Carnival cake balls

› 400 g of flour; 4 eggs;
› 100 g of butter; 50 g of sugar;
› 1 shot of rum;
› the zest of 1 lemon;
› 100 g of powdered sugar mixed with powdered cinnamon;
› salt and extra virgin olive oil to taste.

 QUICK   EASY

THE HISTORY OF THE DISH

This is the Roman version of a classic Carnival treat that exists in different variants throughout the peninsula. It is not the lightest of desserts ... but Carnival only comes once a year!

DIRECTIONS

Put the flour in a large mixing bowl and add the beaten eggs, the melted rum, the butter, the grated lemon zest and a pinch of salt. Knead the dough until it becomes soft and smooth. Make balls the size of a chestnut and then fry them a few at a time in a large pan of boiling oil. As soon as they have risen and turned golden brown, remove them from the oil and allow them to drain on paper towels to eliminate any excess oil. Dust with powdered sugar and cinnamon powder and place them on a serving dish. They are also good served cold.

TRADITIONAL RESTAURANTS

MATRICIANELLA

› Via del Leone, 4 (Piazza di Spagna)
› Tel.: 06 6832100
  info@matricianella.it - www.matricianella.it
› Closed: Sundays
› Average price (excluding drinks):
  Euro 40,00

There are many strong points at Matricianella: the location (just steps away from the Spanish Steps and Trinità dei Monti), the high quality wines, the choice ingredients and the cuisine, which fully mirrors Roman tradition.
The environment is friendly and the service is efficient. The tables are a little close together, but that is also very Roman. Specialties: lamb, amatriciana-style pasta, codfish, carbonara-style pasta, artichokes, oxtail stew, zucchini flowers, gricia-style pasta, "puntarelle" chicory salad, "supplì" rice croquettes

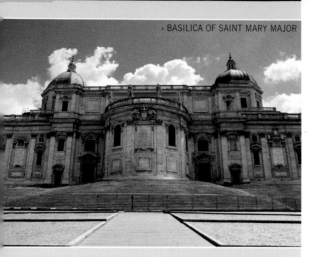

TRADITIONAL RESTAURANTS

LA MATRICIANA

› Via del Viminale, 44 (S. Maria Maggiore)
› Tel.: 06 4881775
  www.lamatriciana.it
  info@lamatriciana.it
› Closed: Saturdays
› Average price (excluding drinks): Euro 35,00

"La Matriciana" restaurant is just a few minutes from St. Mary Major right in front of the Teatro dell'Opera. It was founded in the same year as the Italian Republic in 1870 (it is part of the Historical Establishments of Italy Association).
The environment seems to recall old-fashioned Rome and the cuisine is truly authentically Roman.
Specialties: lamb, amatriciana-style pasta, ricotta pie, gricia-style pasta, "puntarelle" chicory salad

Crostata di ricotta

Ricotta cheese pie

› 450 g of pasta frolla (recipe below);
› 400 g of ricotta;
› 200 g of sugar;
› 50 g of dark chocolate in flakes or chips;
› 3 eggs;
› orange zest, candied fruits, rum and cinnamon to taste.

THE HISTORY OF THE DISH

Due to the local production of great sheep ricotta, the pastry chefs in Lazio used it as a filling for a magnificent crostata which can be made with various additions and flavours.
This is the original version from Upper Lazio.

DIRECTIONS

Beat the ricotta and eggs (2 whole eggs and 1 yolk) and all of the other ingredients. Roll out a round circle of pasta frolla and turn up the edges to make a pie crust and place it in a buttered pie pan, then add the filling and smooth it. With the remaining pasta frolla make small strips and lay them crosswise over the ricotta, and then brush the dough with egg white. Bake at 180° for around 45 minutes and once it has cooled sprinkle with powdered sugar.

PASTA FROLLA (Italian shortbread crust) RECIPE
Ingredients: 200 g of flour; 100 g of sugar; 100 g of butter; 2 egg yolks; grated lemon zest and a pinch of salt. Pour the flour into a mixing bowl and make a cone shape with a hole at the centre. Place the other ingredients in the hole of the cone (the butter needs to be softened first). Knead well and let the dough rest for around half an hour. Press it into a baking pan (carefully, because the dough tends to break and therefore this step requires a little patience).

RECOMMENDED WINE

EST! EST!! EST!!! DI MONTEFIASCONE (DOC)

This wine is produced in Montefiascone, a hilltop town in the Tuscia area just a few kilometres from Viterbo and near Bolsena Lake. The wine tradition in Montefiascone dates back to ancient times as is evidenced by its name (in Italian 'fiasco' refers to the classic flasks which were used to hold the wine) and the ancient coat of arms showing images of the wine barrels. There is a famous legend that tells of the origin of the name which dates to the year 1111: a German bishop named Monsignor Deulk, who was in the entourage of Henry V, was travelling to Rome. A great wine enthusiast, he had his quartermaster Martin scout out ahead to taste the local wines and indicate the best ones. The agreement was that his servant would mark the quality inns with the writing EST (which meant 'it is') to mean that 'here it is good'. Enthralled by Montefiascone, Martin marked the local inn with an enthusiastic EST! EST!! EST!!! The innkeeper liked the name and continued to call it that and since then this has been the name of Montefiascone wine. It makes a perfect dinner wine which is at its best with freshwater fish and light appetizers. The abboccato variety is good with homemade desserts and ricotta cake.

TRADITIONAL RESTAURANTS

SANTOPADRE

› Via Collina, 18 (Porta Pinciana)
› Tel.: 06 4745405
› Closed: Sundays
› Average price (excluding drinks): Euro 45,00

"Santopadre" is located very near the Porta Pinciana gate and it offers a great selection of all the typical Roman dishes with lots of seafood specialties on Friday.
The environment is pleasant, rustic and very welcoming with three rooms decorated with photos, horse paraphernalia and jockeys' jerseys. The menu is based on regional and Roman specialties.
Specialties: lamb, cacio e pepe-style pasta, gricia-style pasta

Frappe

Crispy carnival fritters

	AVERAGE
	QUICK

› 500 g of flour;
› 30 g of shortening;
› 2 egg yolks and 1 whole egg;
› 1 tablespoon of sugar;
› salt, white wine, extra virgin olive oil and powdered sugar to taste.

› THE "TWIN" CHURCHES OF SANTA MARIA DI MONTESANTO AND SANTA MARIA DEI MIRACOLI - PIAZZA DEL POPOLO

THE HISTORY OF THE DISH

These small treats are a traditional
Carnival specialty. They are best when
they are fresh, thin and crispy.

DIRECTIONS

Pour the flour into a bowl and make a
small indention in the centre where
you will add the shortening, the yolks,
the whole egg, the sugar and the salt.
Add white wine and mix until the
dough is elastic but not sticky. Let the
dough rest for a while and then roll
out a sheet of dough (very thin) on a
floured table. Use a serrated cutter to
make zigzag shaped ribbons in the
lengths you prefer: you can make
them simple or with a twist. Fry the
strips oil and shortening and
afterwards lay them on a plate in a
pyramid shape and top them with
oodles of powdered sugar.

RECOMMENDED WINE

ALEATICO DI GRADOLI (DOC)
This wine is produced in a small hilly
zone that faces the northeast bank of
Bolsena Lake in the province of
Viterbo, near the borders of Umbria
and Tuscany. It is made exclusively
from Aleatico grapes, which were
introduced to Italy from Greece in the
ancient era of the Etruscans. The
production area of this particular
grape variety has not expanded due to
the fact that the land and
microclimate of this area are uniquely
ideal for its growth, making Aleatico di
Gradoli an excellent and rare product.
Aleatico is best with cookies, sweets
made from marzipan; pies and
traditional desserts.

Maritozzi

Roman sweet buns

› 500 g of raised bread dough;
› 20 g of pine nuts;
› 20 g of raisins;
› 3 tablespoons of powdered sugar;
› 3 tablespoons of extra virgin olive oil;
› orange zest to taste.

 MEDIUM   EASY

THE HISTORY OF THE DISH

Traditionally a dessert served during Lent, the
Maritozzo then became a typical breakfast
sweet, without the addition of the traditional
pine nuts. In many Roman cafes you can see
them appetizingly displayed in their most
tasty version: open and overflowing with lots
of whipped cream.

DIRECTIONS

Mix all of the ingredients together with the
dough and quickly knead. Divide the dough
into two small oval buns. Butter a baking pan
and place the dough onto the pan without
letting the buns touch. Let the dough raise
until it has doubled in size. Bake in the oven
at 200° for around 20 minutes. Before
serving, dust with powdered sugar.

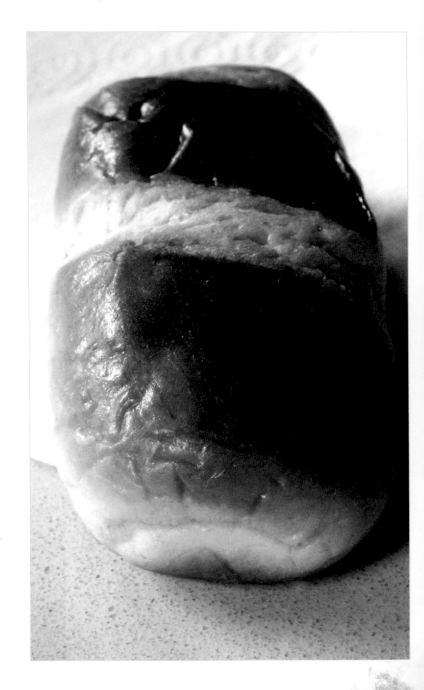

Photo References

The publisher shall comply with envisaged requirements for any photos of unknown origin.

Traditional Restaurants Index

This is a list of all the establishments in the book.
On the previous page a map of the centre of Rome shows
their location.
THESE ARE NOT ADVERTISEMENTS
Please excuse us for any errors or omissions which may
have occurred despite our best intentions.
If you have any comments or suggestions that you think
could improve the publication, please let us know.

Recipe Index

Wine Index